D0055230

The Media and Democracy

John Keane

Polity Press

Copyright © John Keane 1991

First published 1991 by Polity Press
in association with Basil Blackwell

Editorial office:
Polity Press, 65 Bridge Street,
Cambridge CB2 1UR, UK

Marketing and production:
Basil Blackwell Ltd
108 Cowley Road, Oxford OX4 1JF, UK

Basil Blackwell Inc.
3 Cambridge Center
Cambridge, MA 02142, USA

All rights reserved. Except for the quotation of short passages for the
purposes of criticism and review, no part of this publication may be
reproduced, stored in a retrieval system, or transmitted, in any form or
by any means, electronic, mechanical, photocopying, recording or
otherwise, without the prior permission of the publisher.

Except in the United States of America, this book is sold subject to the
condition that it shall not, by way of trade or otherwise, be lent,
resold, hired out, or otherwise circulated without the publisher's prior
consent in any form of binding or cover other than that in which it is
published and without a similar condition including this condition
being imposed on the subsequent purchaser.

ISBN 0 7456 0803 5
ISBN 0 7456 0804 3 (pbk)

The relevant CIP catalogue record for this book is available from the
British Library or the Library of Congress.

Typeset in 12 on 14pt Bembo
by Wearside Tradespools, Fulwell, Sunderland
Printed in Great Britain by
T.J. Press, Padstow, Cornwall

The Media and Democracy

For K. O'N.

The Media and Democracy

Acknowledgements

The publisher and author are grateful to the following for permission to use and for their help in supplying photographs: Rebecca Allison (p. 93); British Film Institute (p. 51); British Museum (p. 1 reproduced by Courtesy of the Trustees of the British Museum, London); Leo Lawson-O'Neil (p. 115); Thames Television and Butterfield, Day, Devito and Hockney (p. 163).

Preface

————————— ❦ —————————

This essay is a guide to rethinking the relationship between the media and democracy. It opens up and explores a cluster of critical questions: where did the modern ideals of freedom from state censorship and 'liberty of the press' originate? Have they been destroyed during the twentieth century by new forms of state censorship, or the emergence of transnational media conglomerates, or the growth of electronic media? Do the new digital technologies, satellite broadcasting and the convergence of broadcasting and telecommunications hinder or help these ideals? Is the free and equal communication of citizens through the media a feasible ideal at the end of the twentieth century?

These questions have been badly neglected both in recent social science and in the high-pressured, breathless world of print and electronic journalism. Political philosophers argue abstractly about the meaning of concepts such as justice, freedom, community and democracy, convinced that the media are either irrelevant to their concerns, ineffectual, trivializing or only to be enjoyed or talked about outside working hours. Sociologists and media researchers analyse audience reactions, genre formations, the ideological effects of corporate media and the cultural impact of the new information technologies. Eccentric intellectuals predict the demise of bookishness and the domination of contemporary life by media mountebanks peddling fast-cut, three-minute culture. Meanwhile, journalists deliver stories to editors and programme-makers negotiate with commissioning editors. Disc-jockeys pump out music. Policymakers concentrate on programme quotas, cross-media ownership issues and the regulation of cable and satellite broadcasting. Yet almost nobody asks basic questions about the relationship between democratic ideals and institutions and the contemporary media. Despite the growing centrality of communications systems in Western democracies – their partial replacement of churches, political parties and trade unions as means of forming and representing opinions – questions about the meaning of freedom and equality of communication cut no ice. They seem ridiculously old fashioned.

The troubling exception to this trend is market liberalism. In recent years, in countries such as the United States, Italy, Germany and Britain, the proponents of 'deregulation' have captured the high ground of public debate about the future of the media. They have powerfully questioned the prevailing mix of public and private means of communication operating within the boundaries of the nation state. Their language has forced a crisis in state-centred interpretations of the media. Their market liberalism sends shivers up the spines of public service broadcasters and state administrators; in the post-communist regimes of such countries as Poland, Hungary and the Czech and Slovak Federal Republic, market liberalism enjoys a stunning rise of popularity. Market liberalism has ensured that public policies concerning the press and especially broadcasting and telecommunications are shaped increasingly by old-fashioned talk of state censorship, individual choice, deregulation and market competition. It forecasts the dawning of an age of communications marked by 'freedom and choice, rather than regulation and scarcity' (Rupert Murdoch).

This essay also engages and criticizes such claims. It traces their origins in the early modern struggles for 'liberty of the press' against state despotism. It shows how the contemporary market liberal case for freedom of communication is spoiled by its fetish of 'market competition', which always produces market censorship and usually leaves untouched the problem of political censorship. This essay throws fresh light on the profoundly disturbing growth of unaccountable 'government by moonlight' in all Western democracies, and it proposes new ways of restricting these new state mechanisms for powerfully regulating and distorting the production and exchange of opinions among citizens. It also charts the long-term and irreversible decline of public service media. It questions the conventional twentieth-century justifications of public service media – for example, that they constitute a 'natural monopoly', or that they are the standard-bearers of 'balanced' or 'quality' programming. But, in opposition to market liberalism, it offers no requiem for public service media. Extending the arguments of my earlier *Public Life and Late Capitalism* and *Democracy and Civil Society*, it sketches a radically new public service model which would facilitate a genuine commonwealth of forms of life, tastes and opinions. Communications media, it is argued, should aim to empower a plurality of citizens who are governed neither by undemocratic states nor by undemocratic market forces. The media should be for the public use and enjoyment of all citizens and not for the private gain or profit of political rulers or businesses.

This new model of public service communications has profound implications for the ways in which we have thought about the media and democracy. It acknowledges the point that in large-scale societies representative structures of communication cannot be bypassed; and that – analogous to representative government – the dangers of irresponsible communication permanently threaten democratic societies. It also forces a reconsideration of the famous American First Amendment ('Congress shall make no law . . . abridging the freedom of speech or of the press') and activates the need for new methods of exposing and controlling unaccountable state power. This essay shows how a revised public service model also requires the development of a plurality of non-state and non-market media that function as permanent thorns in the side of state power, and serve as the primary means of communication for citizens living within a diverse and horizontally organized civil society. And emphasis is given to the democratic potential of the new microelectronic technologies, which strengthen the hand of individual reception and 'narrowcasting' against conventional broadcasting patterns, and 'socialize' certain tools of communication by encouraging the perception of communication as complex *flows of opinion* through networks of public spheres, rather than as discrete commodities which can be privately owned and controlled, and marketed as profitable things.

Finally, this essay continues my life-long preoccupation with democracy. It proposes a new, non-foundationalist understanding of the relationship between democracy and the media. Bent on stimulating the contemporary democratic imagination, it provides undogmatic arguments for the compatibility and superiority of democratic procedures and public service communications. It points to the advantages – and potentially dangerous effects – of a revised public service model in societies plagued by 'risks'. It demonstrates how 'freedom of communication' comprises a bundle of (potentially) conflicting component freedoms. And it proposes that freedom and equality of communication is not something which can be realized in a definitive sense. Should pornography be curbed or banned outright? Does the state have legal rights to define 'seditious libel'? To what extent should the funding of media be tied to commercial advertising? How can citizens best exercise their powers of reply against their media representatives? Are there occasions where freedom of expression serves to reduce freedom of expression? Questions of this kind, this essay suggests, cannot be made to disappear in democratic societies. The subject of democracy and the media must forever remain open and controversial. The fight for a democratic media is an ongoing project without ultimate solutions. It is a fight for a type of society which is bound to produce more than its share of dissenters, because it is endowed with more than its due of conscientious objection to infallibility.

I am grateful to Nicholas Garnham, Jürgen Habermas, Paul Mier and Nancy Wood for their long-standing support for my attempts to think through these themes.

London
December 1990

Liberty of the Press

Were it left to me to decide whether we should have a Government without Newspapers, or Newspapers without a Government, I should not hesitate a moment to prefer the latter.

Thomas Jefferson, 1787

On a drizzly mid-December morning in 1792, Thomas Paine, citizen extraordinary and author of *Rights of Man*, was brought to trial *in absentia* at the Guildhall in London, charged with propagating 'seditious libel'. A 'special jury' had been hand-picked for the occasion. According to reports, the jury members, all plump, wealthy and respectable men, were filled with icy hostility towards Paine. The recent revolutionary events in France had left them in a state of deep shock. Probably their noses could smell the blood of the September massacres; their brains were pressed by thoughts of the King's coming trial; and their ears still echoed with the cries of plebeians storming the Bastille and the taunts trailing the King's slow march from Versailles to the Tuileries.

The charge against Tom Paine was introduced to the court by the Honourable Spencer Perceval (who seventeen years later was to become Prime Minister of England). Paine was described as a traitor to his country, as a drunken roisterer who had actively supported both the American and French Revolutions and who had vilified Parliament, king and the precious settlement of 1688. The courtroom hushed. Perceval began: 'Thomas Paine late of London, . . . being a wicked, malicious, seditious, and ill-disposed person . . . and most . . . seditiously and maliciously . . . contriving and intending to . . . traduce and vilify the late happy revolution providentially brought about . . . under . . . His Highness William, heretofore Prince of Orange, and afterwards King of England . . . did write and publish . . . a certain false . . . seditious libel of and concerning the said late happy revolution . . . and . . . our present Lord the king . . . and . . . the parliament of this kingdom, entitled *Rights of Man, Part the Second.'*

Shortly after Perceval's summary of the charge, Thomas Erskine, Attorney General to the Prince of Wales, rose to his feet to defend Tom Paine. Erskine's task was virtually impossible. The prosecution and jury were deeply hostile, and even before the trial had begun Erskine himself had been pilloried throughout the Tory press as a Paineite and fellow traveller of the French Revolution. But Erskine was renowned as a brilliant legal mind. He was also an eloquent orator who liked to deliver long addresses. This one on 18 December 1792 was no exception. It lasted more than four hours. Each word was recorded painstakingly by Joseph Gurney, the principal shorthand writer in London at that time, and the whole text was later published in several editions, which are today deposited in the vaults of the British Library.[1]

Summarized, Erskine's argument was that the charge of seditious libel against Paine was unjustified because it violated a key principle of the British constitution – the principle of the liberty of the press. Erskine attacked the

---

[1] *The Celebrated Speech of the Hon. T. Erskine in Support of the Liberty of the Press* (Edinburgh, 1793). All page numbers in the text refer to this edition.

view, defended by Sir William Blackstone and Chief Justice Mansfield, and by Tory writers like Jonathan Swift and Dr Johnson, that Parliament is always the sovereign power. Erskine criticized the principle of the sovereignty of official state politics. He came close to accepting the First Amendment to the United States Constitution (15 December 1791), which specified that 'Congress shall make no law . . . abridging the freedom of speech or of the press.' In matters of publishing, Erskine argued, Parliament's power is limited by the right of individuals freely to speak and to publish their views. Each individual naturally requires the oxygen of publicity. The government of citizens' tongues, brains and eyes is inadmissible. Liberty of the press is an imprescriptible natural right, given by God. It cannot be infringed by any earthly power, and certainly not by corrupt governments wanting to save their own skins. The right to a free press is a political trump held by individuals against government. 'Every man', Erskine emphasized, 'may analyze the principles of its constitution, point out its errors and defects, examine and publish its corruptions, warn his fellow citizens against their ruinous consequences' (p. 13). Erskine went farther. Echoing Paine, he implied that all individuals are duty-bound to respect their fellows' natural right of free expression. And he denied that the free exercise of this natural right by means of a free press would lead to rebellion and disorder. Civil disputes conducted in ink would not end in bloody civil war. On the contrary, rapacious governments are the prime cause of civil disorder, whereas government based on public discussion among citizens with a conscience is naturally peaceful, if noisy. A free press, like the spear of Telephus, could heal the wounds it inflicts upon the body politic: 'Let men communicate their thoughts with freedom, and their indignation fly off like a fire spread on the surface; like gunpowder scattered, they kindle, they communicate; but the explosion is neither loud nor dangerous: keep them under restraint, it is subterranean fire, whose agitation is unseen till it bursts into earthquake or volcano' (pp. 46–7).

These arguments left the jury cold. The prosecution rose to reply, but Mr Campbell, the foreman of the jury, interrupted to explain that he had been instructed by his brother jurors to save time by delivering an immediate verdict – of guilty. According to reports, several people in the courtroom instantly hissed the verdict. Cries of 'Take them into custody' were heard. Panic ensued. The friends of Erskine, who had received many anonymous threatening letters prior to the trial, feared for his life. They bustled him out on to the steps of the Guildhall where, to everybody's surprise, a crowd of several thousand supporters had gathered, chanting 'Erskine for ever!', 'Erskine and the Rights of Juries!' and 'Erskine and the liberty of the press!' Some members of the Whiggish and Radical crowd proposed to unhitch the horses from Erskine's carriage, and to draw him by hand to his home in Serjeant's Inn. Erskine declined the offer. He stated that he was exhausted by the day's business and that he would be most honoured if his kind supporters permitted his horses to remain harnessed to his carriage. His polite request was in vain. The crowd pressed forwards. The horses were unharnessed, the traces were seized and Erskine's carriage was hauled manually through the narrow streets, amidst loud applause. As the procession entered Cheapside, the crowd swelled. The street was filled with more cries of 'Erskine and the Liberty of the Press'. Windows were flung open. Women, waving handkerchiefs, called out 'God bless you Erskine; God bless you my dear Erskine'. At some windows, and in the street, gentlemen, some of them sober, shouted 'Damn Tom Paine, but Erskine for ever and the Liberty of the Press'. The throng became so great at Fleet market that the procession was detained for fifteen minutes. Eventually it arrived at Serjeant's Inn, which by that time was overflowing with supporters. Erskine alighted from his carriage, made a low bow, and entered his house amidst thunderous applause from the large crowd, which dispersed peaceably within a few minutes.

This tiny anecdote from the history of the struggle for a free press is among the most dramatic from this period, even though it has been touched by the silence of time. Like a worn inscription upon a gravestone in the far corner of an overgrown cemetery, it serves as a reminder of the rich and complex history of early modern attempts to break the padlocks of press censorship. It helps recall the point – emphasized by Ferdinand Tönnies in his pathbreaking work, *Kritik der öffentlichen Meinung*[2] – that the call for press freedom is a

---

[2] *Kritik der öffentlichen Meinung* (Berlin, 1922). Published in the same year as Walter Lippmann's famous *Public Opinion*, Tönnies's work was for many years, at least prior to the victory of Nazism, considered the best European treatise on the subject of the press and public opinion. Unfortunately, it is still largely unknown in the English-speaking world. Tönnies intended to examine the origins and development of the idea of public opinion in a companion volume, only fragments of which were published. See, for example, 'Necker über die öffentliche Meinung', *Zeitungswissenschaft*, vol. 2, n. 6 (1927), pp. 81–2; and the treatment of the eighteenth-century writings of Wieland and Garve in 'Die öffentliche Meinung in unserer Klassik' *Archiv für Buchgewerbe und Graphik*, vol. 65, no. 4 (1928), pp. 31–49.

distinctive organizing principle of the modern European and North American worlds, and that the theory and practice of publicly articulating opinions through media of communication developed endogenously in no other civilization. Admittedly, demands for press freedom were distributed unevenly throughout the European region. No comparative study of this pattern of distribution exists at present. Yet it seems clear that the call for 'liberty of the press' was strongest in western Europe, where the feudal components of the medieval *corpus politicum* relinquished their struggle against state builders only gradually and unwillingly. All European absolutist states strove to subordinate and to 'police' their subjects. But in practice nowhere in western Europe were various negative freedoms and local autonomies eliminated. Not surprisingly, in this region of Europe (especially the Netherlands and England) the lifespan of absolutist states was comparatively brief, and the call for liberty of the press especially loud by European standards. Even so, public arguments about the role of the press took root even in those European countries (such as Spain and Russia) with the lowest literacy rates and most despotic governments.[3] And wherever Europeans settled in the world – in the North American territories, in the colonies of the West Indies, India or Africa – they created media modelled on those at home. Things were radically different in other civilizations. In the Ottoman Empire, for example, printing in Turkish or Arabic was banned completely until 1727; the single printing establishment created in that year

---

[3] See Gary Marker, *Publishing, Printing, and the Origins of Intellectual Life in Russia, 1700–1800* (Princeton, NJ, 1985); and Paul-J. Guinard, *La presse espagnole de 1737 à 1791* (Paris, 1973).

was suppressed by the political authorities shortly afterwards, not to be reopened until 1784.[4] In Japan, the extensive broadsheet and pamphlet press of the Tokugawa period was largely apolitical and subjected to tight censorship; news periodicals first appeared in that country only during the 1860s, under the influence of Western models.[5] And in China, where periodical newssheets appeared for the first time anywhere in the world, perhaps as early as the eighth century, the press was considered exclusively a tool for enhancing the power and legitimacy of the ruling bureaucracies.[6]

In the European context, the long and drawn-out fight for 'liberty of the press' appeared first and most vigorously in Britain (from where it spread rapidly to America and, less energetically, to the Continent).[7] The landmarks of the British struggle are well documented. It commenced with the English Revolution, which overturned and set fire to old ways of life, and produced

---

[4] Bernard Lewis, *The Emergence of Modern Turkey* (London, 1961), p. 51.

[5] Albert Altman, '"Shimbunshi": The Early Meiji Adaptation of the Western-style Newspaper', in William G. Beasley (ed.), *Modern Japan: Aspects of History, Literature and Society* (Berkeley, Cal., 1975), pp. 52, 56.

[6] Lin Yutang, *A History of the Press and Public Opinion in China* (New York, 1968), p. 12.

[7] On the development of struggles for liberty of the press in Britain and the United States, see Jeremy Black, *The English Press in the Eighteenth Century* (Philadelphia, 1987); Leonard Levy, *Emergence of a Free Press* (New York, 1985); Bernard Bailyn and John B. Hench (eds), *The Press and the American Revolution* (Worcester, Mass., 1980); F. S. Siebert, *Freedom of the Press in England 1476–1776. The Rise and Decline of Government Control* (Urbana, Ill., 1965); and W. H. Wickwar, *The Struggle for the Freedom of the Press, 1819–1832* (London, 1928).

Milton's *Areopagitica*, William Walwyn's *The Compassionate Samaritane* and scores of other breathtaking tracts in defence of press freedom. The political flux and intellectual sting of that period was deepened by the confluence of relatively cheap and portable printing presses and Leveller writers, printers and hawkers, at a time when printing was still a small man's occupation, and not yet a capitalist industry. The long revolution in favour of a free press included the subsequent collapse of the cumbersome licensing system inherited by William and Mary and the expiry of the Regulation of Printing Act in 1694. This act of 'deregulation' continued to treat the publication of blasphemous, seditious, obscene or defamatory material as a criminal offence. But it formally sanctioned the liberty to print all material and paved the way for the appearance of the first daily newspaper, the *Daily Courant* (1702).

The resistance to state control of the media nevertheless continued. It was boosted by the daring and influential defence of freedom of expression during the 1720s by 'Cato' (John Trenchard and Thomas Gordon). It was widened by the successful campaign of John Wilkes, during the reign of George III, to use the newspapers publicly to defend himself as a member of Parliament against charges of seditious libel and blasphemy, and thereby to legitimate the open reporting of Parliamentary proceedings by the press. In two major court cases during the 1760s, *Leach* v. *Money* and *Entick* v. *Carrington*, the legal authority of governments to issue general warrants was abolished; after that time, the state was no longer authorized to arrest any person suspected of having a hand in the publication of seditious libel, or to search the homes and offices of suspected persons or to seize any incriminating papers which might be found. A

stamp tax on American newspapers, pamphlets, advertisements, almanacks and calendars in the American
colonies was repealed in 1766, after violent opposition.
Huge interest in the subject of liberty of the press was
aroused by the pamphlet war inspired by the French
Revolution. During the 1780s and 1790s, Mary Wollstonecraft, Tom Paine, Richard Price, William Godwin
and others depicted the ruling orders as parasites,
pilferers, indolents, incompetents and miscreants. They
synthesized popular vocabularies with popular suspicion of the governing class, thereby contributing to the
formation of a more democratic press which regarded
politics as the business of every citizen, male and female,
rich and poor. This popular agitation preceded all the
momentous reforms of the first half of the nineteenth
century, such as the abolition of slavery and the slave
trade, the enfranchisement of the middle classes and the
repeal of the Corn Laws. It reached feverish heights in
the active resistance of the pauper press to state censorship by regulation, price and taxes on knowledge – a
resistance embodied in the unstamped newspapers of
the 1830s with titles like the *Destructive*, the *Poor Man's
Guardian* and the *Red Republican*, which were smuggled
out of London's grimy backstreet print shops to all parts
of the country in coffins, hatboxes and baskets covered
with apples, bread or dirty laundry.

The philosophy of press freedom

> *People ask if liberty of the press is advantageous or prejudicial
> to a state.*
>
> Louis, Chevalier de Jaucourt, 1753

The extended Euro-American revolution in support of
'liberty of the press' fuelled, especially during the

eighteenth century, a salmagundi of innovative and sophisticated arguments about the proper scope of state censorship. These philosophical discourses in favour of freedom of expression, publishing and reading are rarely analysed nowadays. They are mostly out of print and largely forgotten. They almost never appear in political science or communications textbooks, despite the fact that they are among the richest and most exciting political discourses of the early modern period. Those who argued for snapping the padlocks of state censorship relied upon a variety of sophisticated claims. In Britain, the birthplace of the modern principle of liberty of the press, at least four different (if sometimes overlapping) species of argument are discernible. They are well worth deciphering, since they help to prepare a case for a forward-looking political theory of the media with eyes in the back of its head:

(1) The *theological* approach criticized state censorship in the name of the God–given faculty of reason enjoyed by individuals. It flourished in many English Civil War tracts, such as Henry Burton's *A Vindication of the Churches Commonly Called Independent* (1644), Henry Robinson's *Liberty of Conscience* (1644) and William Walwyn's *The Compassionate Samaritane* (1644). It is expounded most eloquently in John Milton's *Areopagitica* (1644).[8]

In defiance of a government order requiring the licensing and censorship of books, Milton pleaded for a free press in order to let the love of God and the 'free and knowing spirit' flourish. Milton argued that blanket

---

[8] All citations are drawn from *Areopagitica. A Speech for the Liberty of Unlicenc'd Printing*, E. H. Visiak (ed.), *Milton. Complete Poetry and Selected Prose* (Glasgow, 1925).

restrictions upon the press are inefficient and unworkable (likening them to the foolish actions of the 'gallant man who thought to pound up the crows by shutting his Parkgate' [p. 698]). Press censorship is also repugnant because it stifles the exercise of individuals' freedom to think, to exercise discretion, and to opt for a Christian life. Censors – who are by no means graced with 'infallibility and uncorruptedness' – cannot decide for us how we are to live. God loaned individuals reason and, hence, the capacity to read and to choose, according to the dictates of conscience, between good and evil. God reveals his trust in us by directing us to read any books we wish and to judge them for ourselves. The keys of the press have been bequeathed us out of paradise. That is why Milton railed against the cloistering of reason. The virtue of individuals must be developed and tested continually by engaging contrary opinions and experiences. Virtue cannot depend on innocence, since good and evil are intertwined: 'it is not possible for man to sever the wheat from the tares, the good fish from the other frie; that must be the Angels Ministry at the end of mortall things' (p. 723). Evil exists to exercise the good. Blasphemy and libel cohabit with truth. Good can be known only through familiarity with evil. The toleration of different and conflicting opinions is thus a basic condition of individual discretion and virtue: 'that which purifies us is triall, and triall is by what is contrary' (p. 696).

Milton was not in favour of full freedom of the press from state regulation. He insisted that the books of popish bigots should be expurgated, and that in the fight for virtue toleration of the intolerant would be self-defeating. He reserved the law of subsequent punishment for any abuse or licentiousness of the press. Yet he had no doubt that the general suppression of published opinions is evil. It wrongly supposes that knowledge of good and evil is a dutiable commodity. It treats individuals as if they were giddy and vicious. It lowers the dignity of a nation. It demonstrates no faith in the power of the clergy to resist false doctrines. State censorship rejects God's gift of reason to man. It is a form of homicide: 'who kills a Man kills a reasonable creature, Gods Image; but hee who destroyes a good Booke, kills reason it selfe, kills the Image of God, as it were in the eye [that is, as reflected directly in the human mind]' (p. 687).

(2) The idea that the conduct of the press should be guided by the *rights of individuals* is sketched in John Locke's *Epistola de tolerantia ad clarissimum virum* (1689) and is developed explicitly in John Asgill's *An Essay for the Press* (1712). It is evident in the remarkable series of articles by 'Cato' (John Trenchard and Thomas Gordon), *The Independent Whig* (1720) and *Cato's Letters* (1720–3); in Thomas Hayter's *An Essay on the Liberty of the Press, Chiefly as It Respects Personal Slander* (1758); and in an anonymous tract, *An Essay on the Right of Every Man in a Free State to Speak and Write Freely, in Order to Defend the Public Rights, and Promote the Public Welfare: and on Various Great Occasions for the Present Use of It* (1772). Its popularity was fuelled by the constitutional innovations of the American and French Revolutions, and by deeply controversial texts such as Tom Paine's *Rights of Man* (1791–2) and Mary Wollstonecraft's *Vindication of the Rights of Woman* (1792).

The natural-rights theory of press freedom was first developed explicitly in Matthew Tindal's *Reasons Against Restraining the Press* (1704).[9] Tindal dismissed

---

[9] All citations are drawn from the first edition, Matthew Tindal, *Reasons Against Restraining the Press* (London, 1704).

religious justifications of press censorship. Those who
yearn for theocratic rule are 'pious frauds and holy
cheats'. They long to fling their subjects into 'Egyptian
bondage' on the basis of a mistaken understanding of
Christianity. In language reminiscent of Milton, Tindal
insisted that we are rational creatures with God-given
capacities for deciding the truth of opinions. But he
went further, turning in another direction, grounding
his claims on 'the natural right everyone has of judging
for himself in matters of religion' (pp. 288–9). Restrictions on the press are un-Christian and contrary to
natural right. 'The noble art of printing, that by divine
providence was discovered to free men from the tyranny of the clergy they then groaned under, . . . ought not
to be made a means to reduce us again under sacerdotal
slavery' (p. 288).

Tindal then extended the same natural-right principle
from the religious to the political sphere. Individuals
who are endowed with natural rights in matters of
religious belief cannot be expected to abandon them at
the gates of state power. Throughout Europe, states
currently silence their subjects with 'court language'.
Equipped with 'dependents, ready upon all occasions to
write in justification of their conduct', states 'gild over
the worst of their actions, and give a fair colour to their
most pernicious designs' (p. 296). Against this trend,
there is a natural tendency of individuals to publish 'by
stealth' against state restrictions. This is right and
proper, Tindal argued, for individuals are entitled to
exercise their natural rights freely against governments.
Principal among these rights is liberty of the press. 'Like
a faithful centinel', a free press 'prevents all surprize, and
gives timely warning of any approaching danger'
(p. 298). Press freedom is a guarantee of freedom from

political coxcombs, Parliamentary hoodwinking and governmental slavery. It ensures good government, based on the natural rights of rational individuals who are capable of living, together with their elected representatives, under the rule of law.

(3) The theory of *utilitarianism* viewed state censorship of public opinion as a licence for despotism and as contrary to the principle of maximizing the happiness of the governed. William Godwin's *Enquiry Concerning Political Justice* (1798) and James Mill's *Liberty of the Press* (1811) contain some ingredients of this theory. The argument for 'good government' through 'liberty of the press, and the liberty of public discussion by word of mouth' is developed most thoroughly in Jeremy Bentham's letters to Spanish readers, *On the Liberty of the Press and Public Discussion* (1820–1).[10] Bentham urged that the best governments and laws are those which produce the greatest happiness of the greatest number of people. The key political problem is to develop a system of choosing and authorizing 'undespotic' governments, that is, sets of legislators and law-enforcers who secure the kinds of law which maximize happiness.

A good political system is required to do two things in particular: to produce governments which nurture happiness among citizens by means of a civil society structured by laws and free-market exchanges, *and* to protect those same citizens from rapacious governments. Bentham was convinced that governments are always ruled by self-interest: 'Such is the nature of man when clothed with power . . . that . . . whatever mischief has not yet been actually done by him to-day, he is

---

[10] All citations are drawn from Jeremy Bentham, *On the Liberty of the Press and Public Discussion* (London, 1820–1).

sure to be meditating to-day, and unless restrained by the fear of what the public may think and do, it may actually be done by him to-morrow' (p. 15). This maxim is confirmed in England and Spain, Bentham explained. In those countries, the aristocracy, in collaboration with the monarchy, does what it pleases. The aristocratic class is 'an alliance defensive and offensive against the interest of the people: of the ruling one and the sub-ruling few against the subject many' (p. 17).

Despotism of this kind – 'the thirst for arbitrary power' – could be checked, as had happened already in the United States, by mechanisms such as a broadened franchise, secret ballots and frequent elections. Especially important is press freedom, since without it elections could not be considered free and effective expressions of the voters' wishes. Periodic elections without continuous press freedom would resemble a farm on which 'for eight months in the year, all sheep dogs were to be kept locked up, and the sheep committed during that time to the guardianship of the wolves' (p. 18). Hence, the utilitarian case for liberty of the press is that it serves as a counterweight to despotic government – as a 'check upon the conduct of the ruling few'. It thereby facilitates the making and application of laws supportive of the greatest satisfaction of the greatest number. A free press is the ally of happiness. It helps to control the 'habitual self-preference' of those who govern. It exposes their secretiveness and makes them more inclined to respect and to serve the governed. It increases the probability of prudent decisions by making publicly available comprehensive information about the world. And a free press casts a watchful public eye over the bureaucracy, thus preventing the outbreak of nepotism between legislators and administrators.

Like Erskine and others before him, Bentham rejected the view that press freedom leads to insurrection and civil war. Unhappiness is never the child of press freedom: 'In all liberty, there is more or less of danger . . . and so there is in all power' (p. 11). Good government supposes the effective capacity publicly to criticize, resist and remove the government of the day. Liberty of the press maximizes happiness among the governed. In political life, happiness is a prize in a zero-sum game: the more the minority of governors have, the less the governed majority enjoy.

(4) A fourth defence of liberty of the press is guided by the idea of attaining *Truth* through unrestricted public discussion among citizens. Early modern English tracts on tolerance and the press hint at this idea. An early example is to be found in Leonard Busher's tract, *Religion's Peace: or, a Plea for liberty of conscience* (1614): 'Even as the Chaff before the Wind cannot stand, so Error before Truth cannot abide.' Truth-grounded arguments for liberty of the press developed strongly in Britain during the eighteenth century. Joseph Priestley's *An Essay on the First Principles of Government; and on the nature of political, civil and religious liberty* (1768) is an example. The most influential and secular version appears in the following century: John Stuart Mill's *On Liberty* (1859).[11]

This essay complained that the utilitarian theory of press freedom is symptomatic of an age (Mill quotes Thomas Carlyle) which is 'destitute of faith but terrified at scepticism'. Utilitarianism reinforces the assumption

---

[11] All citations are drawn from John Stuart Mill, *On Liberty*, in J. M. Robson (ed.), *Essays on Politics and Society* (Toronto and Buffalo, 1977), pp. 213–310.

that people are entitled to feel sure, not that their opinions are true, but that they could not live without them, and that these opinions have a self-evident utility. Utilitarianism talks too little about truth and too much about utility, which is itself a matter of opinion and therefore requires rigorous, truth-seeking investigation. The truth of an opinion is an essential part of its utility. Mill pursued a case for the education and improvement of individuals – for 'the necessity to the mental well-being of mankind (on which all their other well-being depends) of freedom of opinion, and freedom of the expression of opinion' (pp. 257–8). He offered three reasons why the guarantee of freely circulating opinion through the press is essential.

First, any opinion which is silenced by government or civil society because it is allegedly false may prove to be true, in the sense that it may conform to the facts and survive vigorous counter-arguments about those facts. Those who seek to censor potentially true opinion naturally deny its truth. But in so doing they make the unwarranted assumption that *their* certainty is equivalent to *absolute* certainty. They suppose their own views about the world to be true, when in fact they normally express their own particular standpoint within the terms of a party, sect, church or social class. To assume infallibility is to suppress potential truth. It is to decide the truth of an opinion for others, without allowing them to hear or digest counter-arguments.

Second, though an opinion turns out to be false, it often contains an ounce or two of truth. The prevailing opinion on any matter is rarely the whole truth. This means that it is only by confronting it with other, contrary opinions that the full truth can be attained. In public affairs, truth necessitates combining and reconciling opposites. 'When there are persons to be found, who form an exception to the apparent unanimity of the world on any subject, even if the world is in the right, it is always probable that dissentients have something worth hearing to say for themselves, and that truth would lose something by their silence' (p. 254).

Mill argued, finally, that even if an opinion is the whole truth, and nothing but the truth, it will soon degenerate into prejudice – into a 'dead dogma, not a living truth' (p. 245) – if it goes unchallenged. 'The fatal tendency of mankind to leave off thinking about a thing when it is no longer doubtful, is the cause of half their errors' (p. 250). Partly this is because historical epochs are no less fallible than individuals or groups. Truth is timeless. The living nevertheless have a bad habit of valuing themselves too highly, and always deem false and absurd some opinions of the dead. The living are bound to suffer this fate at the hands of their offspring: 'it is as certain that many opinions, now general, will be rejected by future ages, as it is that many, once general, are rejected by the present' (p. 230). Truth can also degenerate into prejudice if it is not exercised by counter-claims. Heretics become reticent. Matters are made worse when prejudice cramps and cows of the mental development of others. The practice of learning the grounds and meaning of one's own opinions fades. The 'deep slumber of a decided opinion' then overpowers the moral courage and dignity of the human mind.

Mill's *On Liberty* did not consider that there are many instances of artistic, ethical and political expression which have purposes and consequences other than the discovery of truth such as to entertain, shock, praise, condemn or inspire. *On Liberty* also brushed aside the suggestion that there is a plurality of incommensurable truths, or that their protagonists cannot live together peacefully. The evils of sectarianism can be eradicated by cautious and calm discussion which shuns 'unmeasured vituperation' (p. 259). Sectarianism can also be minimized by prohibiting expressions which cause harm to others: 'No one pretends that actions should be as free as opinions. On the contrary, even opinions lose their immunity when the circumstances in which they are expressed are such as to constitute their expression a positive instigation to some mischievous act' (p. 260). Mill nevertheless doubted the comfortable dictum that in the end truth always wins out against persecution. History teems with examples of suppressed truth. Truth has no inherent power to prevail against the dungeon, the stake or the arrogant censor. Truth requires liberty of the press as its ally. No special laws should exist to hamper the freedom of newspapers, journals, books and pamphlets to print facts and advance opinions. Only a free press can guarantee that there is an abundant supply of facts and arguments about the facts, thus cultivating the habit of questioning and correcting opinions and ensuring the victory of Truth over falsehood.

Despotism

This liberty to grumble and complain about the established government is an inexhaustible source of trouble and revolutions.

Dubois de Launay, 1786

These various arguments in favour of 'liberty of the press' harbour certain difficulties – discussed shortly – and yet, as the trial of Tom Paine reminds us, they profoundly influenced the course of early modern societies. Tönnies's *Kritik der öffentlichen Meinung* is again helpful in exploring this point. Tönnies criticized his contemporaries for overlooking the fundamental significance of the development of 'public opinion' by means of a free press. Modern societies, in his view, are differentiated and associational (*gesellschaftlich*) and structured by three overlapping organizing principles: markets, states and public opinion. Rationally calculated market contracts replace the close-knit household unions (*Eintracht*) of pre-modern communities. Laws formulated through the state (*Gesetzgebung*) replace the rustic folkways and mores of custom (*Sitte*). And public opinion erodes the medieval faith in religion. 'In recent centuries, the Christian religion has lost what public opinion has gained.'[12] In modern times, public opinion expressed through an independent free press breaks down the dark, unreasonable secrecy of 'unproven imaginings, beliefs or authority'.[13] The dominant, collectively shared opinions of modern societies are no longer describable (in the words of Tönnies) as an 'essential will' (*Wesenwille*) comprising dogmatic beliefs and traditional sentiments. The rise of a free press breaks down dogmatic traditions. It fosters reflexiveness. It stimulates the growth of an arbitrary or 'conventional will' (*Kurwille*), that is, publicly decided judgements about desirable goals and deliberate calculations about the means of achieving them. The growth of public opinion in this sense has deep political implications. States are dragged before the court of public opinion. In the name of the common or public interest,

---

[12] Tönnies, *Kritik der öffentlichen Meinung*, p. 570.
[13] Ibid., pp. 77–8.

the press chides tyrants and malefactors who stifle or evade public opinion. The abuse of political power is exposed publicly. Law-making and law-enforcement are subject to noisy public deliberations. Like a brilliant comet in the dark skies of absolutism, the press and public opinion bring light to the modern world.

Tönnies was right about the long-term political importance of struggles against state regulation of publishing. From the time of the English Revolution, the call for 'liberty of the press' was a vital aspect of the modern democratic revolution. It prompted a search for new, more secular and democratic ways of regarding the modern state in Europe and America. Liberty of the press was the unwanted child of European despotism. If only to satisfy their diplomats, officials and military officers, all early modern European states acknowledged the importance of providing a basic minimum of news about wars, treaties, leadership changes and other public events. Those states which tried strictly to control or to suppress such news became identified as despotic. 'One of the principles of the despotic form of government is to keep the people in ignorance of events in the world in general, and above all of those around them', wrote the Constantinople correspondent of the prestigious *Gazette de Leyde* in 1784. He contrasted the Turkish prohibition on newspapers with the European situation, where 'in most monarchies there is at least a public journal, which keeps the nation informed about current events from the government's point of view.'[14] The rulers of monarchic states expected this to enhance their public image, as Gottlob Benedikt von Schirach, a

---

[14] Cited in Jeremy D. Popkin, *News and Politics in the Age of Revolution* (Ithaca, NY, and London, 1989), p. 251.

leading eighteenth-century journalist, pointed out: 'Everywhere, there has been an increase in publicity about politics, a consequence of the enlightenment of our age . . . and governments enjoy increasing trust as they become more open.'[15]

Events proved otherwise. Governments' sanctioning of a 'public right to know' often backfired. Preambles to important royal edicts grew longer and more explicit in their justification of state policies. Ministers defended themselves by encouraging the circulation of pamphlets and anonymous brochures. Apologists for despotism contradicted their case by reaching for their paper and pens to warn against 'democracy' and 'licentious publishing'. Warring states even referred their claims to the fictive tribunal of the international 'public'.[16] All this encouraged educated publics to campaign *from below* for an end to government which kept its subjects in the dark. This campaign was spearheaded by social groups whose scientific, literary, artistic and religious pursuits placed them at odds with the accumulation of unaccountable state power and the corporate practices and elite privileges which it protected. These groups comprised rentiers, booksellers, journalists, academicians, schoolteachers and others of modest background. Their social position was no longer enmeshed deeply in the world of courts, communities, parishes and guilds. Although they were predominantly 'bourgeois' – in the loose sense that they had at least a little property and

---

[15] See his introductory remarks to Johann Hermann Stoever, *Historisch-statistische Beschreibung der Staaten des teutschen Reichs* (Hamburg, 1785), p. xi.

[16] A suggestive analysis is developed by Joseph Klaits, *Printed Propaganda Under Louis XIV: Absolute Monarchy and Public Opinion* (Princeton, NJ, 1976).

some education – these groups were not primarily entrepreneurial and they were often supported in their activities by elements of the nobility, lower churchmen, the artisanry and even state officialdom.[17] They were also given support by groups willing to play cat-and-mouse with the political authorities. Many of these people have been forgotten, and yet their courage, sacrifice and hard labour ensured that readers were supplied with books, pamphlets and newspapers. These characters included the ragpickers begging at the back doors of the houses of the rich for bits of gentlemen's underwear, ladies' petticoats, old rags and linens and other ingredients of printed matter; the print men who lived rough on the road, travelling between one master printer and printing house to the next; and those who helped to circulate, often at great risk, lovingly produced books, pamphlets and newspapers – shopkeepers, subscription reading-room proprietors, booksellers, country ale-house and coffee-house owners and gin-shop publicans.

All these groups wanted change, which they typically viewed as creating a different set of political arrangements rather than simply altering the way power was exercised within the existing state apparatus. In this sense they constituted (potential) discussing and reading public spheres which attempted to elaborate a 'public opinion' on political matters and to direct this opinion, in the name of the emerging civil society, at the

---

[17] See Raymond Birn, 'Malesherbes and the Call for a Free Press', in Robert Darnton and Daniel Roche (eds), *Revolution in Print. The Press in France* (Berkeley, Cal., Los Angeles and London, 1989), pp. 50–66.

secretive and arbitrary actions of the state.[18] The defence of 'public opinion' through press freedom warned of the dangers of 'despotic' government. Despotism was viewed as a system of concentrated secular power without limits.[19] It was seen to feed upon its own expansion and to thrive upon the blind obedience of its anxious subjects. Despotism outlaws open discussion, by unauthorized persons without explicit permission, of government policies. Government is the *secret du roi*. Despotism thereby reduces public opinion to furtive whispers. It oversteps the limits of legitimate power. It crashes blindly through the world, leaving behind a trail of lawlessness, war, waste and confusion.

---

[18] Compare the different accounts of Jürgen Habermas, *Strukturwandel der Öffentlichkeit. Untersuchungen zu einer Kategorie der bürgerlichen Gesellschaft* (Neuwied, 1962); and John Keane, *Public Life and Late Capitalism* (Cambridge and New York, 1984), chapters 2 and 7. Other treatments of the growth of modern public spheres include Lucien Hölscher, 'Öffentlichkeit', in Otto Brunner, Werner Conze and Reinhart Koselleck (eds), *Geschichtliche Grundbegriffe. Historisches Lexikon zur politisch-sozialen Sprache in Deutschland* (Stuttgart, 1978), vol. 4, pp. 413–67; Günter Lottes, *Politische Aufklärung und plebejisches Publikum: zur Theorie und Praxis des englischen Radikalismus im späten 18. Jahrhundert* (Munich, 1979); James J. Sheehan, 'Wie bürgerlich war der deutsche Liberalismus?', mimeographed lecture, Bielefeld, 1987; J. A. W. Gunn, *Beyond Liberty and Property* (Kingston, Ont., 1983), chapter 7; Keith Michael Baker, 'Politics and Public Opinion under the Old Regime: Some Reflections', in Jack R. Censer and Jeremy D. Popkin (eds), *Press and Politics in Pre-Revolutionary France* (Berkeley, Cal., 1987), pp. 204–46; and Raymond Williams, *The Long Revolution* (London, 1961), pp. 156–213.

[19] See my 'Despotism and Democracy', in John Keane (ed.), *Civil Society and the State. New European Perspectives* (London and New York, 1988), pp. 35–71.

In characterizing the modern state in this way, defenders of press liberty helped give arcane and bossy government a bad name. They rejected the proposition that all government is properly 'obscure and invisible' (Francis Bacon). They helped thereby to transform, perhaps irreversibly, our collective understanding of the meaning of political representation and of the need to draw strict limits upon governmental power. Advocates of press freedom laid a few stones in the foundations of a fully modern conception of active citizenship. They viewed secrecy as a footservant to bad government. They stimulated demands for checking the potentially dangerous power of the modern state in favour of civil society. They tried to ensure that the dynamic interests of civil society be re-presented to the state permanently. In this way they contributed to the preservation and growth of the old European spirit of civic humanism.[20] They saw the world in public terms: they talked seriously of the public good, distrusted the haggling individualism of the market, valued self-restraint, and prized the active commitment of citizens to the commonweal called 'virtue'. They agitated for what the Americans called 'democratic republicanism.'[21] A free press was considered a critical ingredient of politics,

---

[20] See J. G. A. Pocock, *The Machiavellian Moment: Florentine Political Thought and the Atlantic Republican Tradition* (Princeton, NJ, 1975); and Joyce Appleby, 'Republicanism in Old and New Contexts', *William and Mary Quarterly*, third series, 43 (1986), pp. 20–34.

[21] Russell Hanson, '"Commons" and "Commonwealth" at the American Founding: Democratic Republicanism as the New American Hybrid', in Terence Ball and J. G. A. Pocock (eds), *Conceptual Change and the Constitution* (Kansas, 1988).

understood as a precarious balance between rulers and those who are ruled. Democratic republicanism assigned rulers the job of serving the *res publica*, or the commonweal. For their part, the ruled were obliged to exercise vigilance in keeping the rulers from abusing their powers by violating the spirit of the commonweal.

This trend was strongly evident towards the end of the eighteenth century, as the intense public reaction to the trial of Tom Paine shows. Even English gentlemen from the governing parties considered their Constitution to be the pride and envy of the world. William Pitt, for example, boasted that England had taught Europe that the liberty of the press and other civil and political freedoms were the foundation of true greatness, and that so long as England retained these freedoms she would continue to dazzle the world with her exploits. Liberty of the press was considered the birthright of Britons, the queen of the world, the great 'palladium of all the civil, political, and religious rights of an Englishman' (Junius). It was, remarked Blackstone, 'essential to the nature of a free State'. Foreigners sometimes agreed: Hegel regarded freedom of the press ('this conversation of the government with the people') as among the principal strengths of the English; Voltaire praised England as a unique country whose free press encouraged people to think; and according to Montesquieu's *De l'esprit des lois* (1748), the liberty to grumble and to complain through a free press helped to liberate England from the heavy, silent fear of despotism. Press freedom enabled England to become a uniquely modern society, which dissolved the traditional boundaries between stability and disorder, truth and falsity, the real and the possible.

Of course, one should not take such claims at face

value, as Whiggish historians are prone to do.[22] Until the middle of the nineteenth century, in both America and Britain, 'liberty of the press' functioned as a bold and infectious utopian notion. It helped to put the wind up the governing classes. It dramatized the state's restrictions upon freedom of expression. It fuelled the struggle for civil rights and political democracy, and familiarized reading publics with such vital subjects as constitutional reform, the need for representative institutions, and the subordination of women, slaves and others. It stimulated the growth of collective reading groups, like the German *Lesegesellschaften*, which gave poorer citizens access to otherwise unaffordable publications.[23] The utopia of a free press also helped to mobilize successive layers of the subordinated classes, and – through Cobbett's *Twopenny Trash* and similar Radical papers – to increase the number of unenfranchised people involved in public affairs (a trend evident in the campaign to abolish slavery and in the public agitations prior to the 1832 Reform Bill and the repeal of the Corn Laws).

The spread of a free press contributed to (and was facilitated by) dramatic changes in the disposition of texts, which made them more secular and easier to read. The denseness and uninterrupted continuity typical of

---

[22] The Whiggish view that there was 'a transition from official to popular control' of the press during the modern period is evident in Stephen Koss, *The Rise and Fall of the Political Press in Britain* (London, 1990).

[23] See Otto Dann (ed.), *Lesegesellschaften und bürgerliche Emanzipation* (Munich, 1981); and François Furet, *Penser la Revolution française* (Paris, 1978), which emphasizes the importance of the work of Augustin Cochin on reading societies as a seedbed of revolutionary ideas and democratic forms of life.

Renaissance texts was broken down during the seventeenth and eighteenth centuries. The awesome coherence of visually dense divine works was eroded (as Locke and others feared) from within. Publishers subdivided texts into compact and discrete units. White triumphed over black. The page underwent a form of aeration. Paragraphs multiplied and techniques of indentation rendered the order of discourse more visible.[24] This alteration of the form of printing weakened the power of the keepers of literary tradition and assisted the growth of a market for secular literature. It also encouraged the rapid spread of sophisticated reading publics capable of choosing among a panoply of different types of publication, ranging from satirical journals (such as the *Spectator*, published by Richard Steele and Joseph Addison) and women's and fashion magazines to travel diaries, learned journals and philosophical books.[25] Compared with the worlds of the nineteenth and twentieth centuries, stuck together by the telegraph and the railroad, telephones, radios, telefaxes, televisions and satellites, early modern citizens lived in a low-velocity universe of communication. There was nevertheless a marked change in the rhythm of communication during the eighteenth century. The intensive (re-)reading of a small number of texts, usually

---

[24] Bruno Delmas and Henri-Jean Martin, *Histoire et pouvoirs de l'écrit* (Paris, 1988).

[25] See Jack R. Censer and Jeremy D. Popkin, 'Historians and the Press', in Censer and Popkin, *Press and Politics in Pre-Revolutionary France*, pp. 18–20. On the dramatic growth of newspaper reading in the eighteenth-century German states, see Martin Welke, 'Die Legende vom "unpolitischen Deutschen": Zeitungslesen im 18. Jahrhundert als Spiegel des politischen Interesses', *Jahrbuch der Wittheit zu Bremen*, 25 (1981), p. 183.

religious, gave way increasingly to the extensive reading of a wide variety of ever-changing texts. And as
Otto Groth argued, the newspaper press, more than any
other medium of that period, stimulated a public desire
for what is new by 'printing up-to-date information' in
regular, predictable and perishable clumps.[26]

The spread of visually accessible, perishable opinion
and sophisticated reading publics undoubtedly deepened
concern about the need to respect the principle of
tolerating divergent opinions. Tolerance and liberty of
the press (and the associated freedoms of association and
public assembly) were often seen to require each other.
Jonathan Swift's satirical attack on 'the Fanatick Strain,
or Tincture of Enthusiasm'; Edmund Burke's 'Toleration is good for all, or it is good for none'; and Thomas
Jefferson's remark that 'it does me no injury for my
neighbour to say that there are twenty Gods or no God'
were all symptomatic of this trend, in which certain
issues of ultimate importance were seen to be a matter
for the conscience or taste of the individual or sect.[27]
Public agreement on ultimate norms was considered
inessential to a free, civilized society. The demand for a
free press contributed to the spread of the civilizing
process, in which social interaction is marked by the
greater self-restraint of individuals and by their relative
freedom from immediate physical violence, as if a

---

[26] Rolf Engelsing, *Der Bürger als Leser* (Stuttgart, 1974); and
Otto Groth, *Die Zeitung* (Mannheim, 1928), vol. 1, p. 22.
[27] Jonathan Swift, *A Tale of a Tub* (London, 1704); Edmund
Burke, 'Protestant Dissenters' Relief Bill. Speech to the House
of Commons, 7 March 1773', in *The Speeches of the Right
Honourable Edmund Burke*, vol. 1 (London, 1816), p. 157; Tho-
mas Jefferson, 'Notes on the State of Virginia, Query XVII', in
The Complete Jefferson (Freeport, NY, 1969), p. 675.

passionless void somehow binds them to others.[28]

This shift is symbolized in Voltaire's famous attack on intolerance and its 'law of persecution' ('the law of tygers: nay, it is even still more savage, for tygers destroy only for the sake of food, whereas we have butchered one another on account of a sentence or a paragraph'). His *Traité sur la Tolérance* (1763)[29] pleaded support for the civilizing effects of mutually agreed, legally guaranteed freedom of expression. It recounts the parable of a Cantonese mandarin, who one day was disturbed by a noisy argument in the streets between three Christians: a Danish almoner, a Dutch chaplain and a Jesuit. The mandarin summoned the three to explain their dispute. Each Christian put his case, the others all the while pulling faces and shrugging shoulders. The three were eventually dismissed, the mandarin concluding: 'If you expect to have your doctrine tolerated here begin by shewing an example of it to each other.' The advice did not stretch far. As the Jesuit left the premises, he met a Dominican missionary on the doorstep. The two fell quickly into a vicious quarrel about the nature of truth, and a fist fight followed. Informed of this new dispute, the mandarin ordered them both to prison. An official asked the mandarin about the length of the prison term. 'Till they are both agreed', came the reply. 'Then, my lord', said the official, 'they will remain in prison all their days.' The

---

[28] Norbert Elias, 'Violence and Civilization: The State Monopoly of Physical Violence and its Infringement', in John Keane (ed.), *Civil Society and the State. New European Perspectives* (London and New York, 1988), pp. 177–98.

[29] François Marie Arouet de Voltaire, *Traité sur la Tolérance* (Geneva, 1763), section 19.

mandarin softened: 'Well, then, let them stay till they forgive one another.' The official, exasperated, retorted 'That they will never do. I know them very well.' Quipped the mandarin: 'Indeed! Then let it be till they *appear* to do so.'

Despite the gains listed above, the demand for the universal access of all male and female citizens to freely circulating books, newspapers and pamphlets was never realized in practice. Cobbett correctly spotted that the call for full liberty of the press remained a utopia: 'The English Press, instead of enlightening, does, as far as it has any Power, keep the People in Ignorance. Instead of cherishing Notions of Liberty, it tends to the making of the People Slaves; instead of being their Guardian, it is the most efficient Instrument in the Hands of all those who oppress or who wish to oppress Them.'[30] At the time of Paine's trial, for instance, the dissemination of news and public opinion in Britain was not the primary purpose of newspapers such as *The Times* and the *Morning Chronicle*. They were dominated by advertisements, from which the newspapers derived the greater part of their revenue. The circulation of newspapers, books and pamphlets was also extremely limited, and always frustrated in various ways. Newspapers were printed by hand and therefore in small numbers (until 1814, when *The Times* first switched to steam-powered printing). Distribution was hindered by Post Office red tape and jobbery; except at the prohibitive letter-rate of postage, for example, newspapers could leave or enter Britain only when franked by Post Office officials. Matters were made worse by poor road communica-

---

[30] William Cobbett, *Cobbett's Political Register* (London, 11 April 1807), p. 3.

tions (the coach which brought the news of the battle of Waterloo in eighteen hours was considered to have performed a miraculous journey; in the same period, the mail coach journey from London to Leeds took thirty-three hours). And there was widespread illiteracy and poverty among the rural and urban working classes. The reality in Britain was that the audience for most publications was drawn mainly from the educated bourgeoisie, the aristocracy, state officialdom and craftspeople who had the money to pay for reading material and the desire and leisure and physical space to peruse it.

The press was also subject to heavy stamp duties and taxes. Until the mid-nineteenth century, the costs of printed material were inflated by heavy stamp duties. These dated from 1712, when Queen Anne's Tory ministers decided to raise additional revenue (and to strike a blow at the opposition press) by taxing newspapers, pamphlets and advertisements. Strict sabbatarians (who opposed the sale of everything on Sundays except mackerel and milk) denounced the avidity for Sunday reading as a growing threat to public morals. Tradesmen and artisans were accused of neglecting their business in favour of pamphleteering and newspaper reading in the ale-house. Printers, and sometimes their type and papers, were seized and held in custody by virtue of a Secretary's warrant. Newspaper reporters were admitted to Parliament only by sufferance; until 1875, they could be ordered from the gallery at a second's notice. Journalists and hawkers were snooped on and sometimes terrified into compliance and servility. Licences for reading rooms were arbitrarily withdrawn. There were regular seizures of 'mercuries', women who hawked papers as they sang ballads about the streets, and who were sometimes committed, on the order of a justice of the peace, to Bridewell as vagrants for ten days. Children were sent to prison for selling newspapers which they could not read, and yet which the courts subsequently found to be seditious. In the colonies (as foreign observers like Raynal pointed out) public opinions guaranteed by the press were either ignored or brutally suppressed. And at home the governing class of Tories and Whigs remained panicky about the spread of literacy and the popular press. Lord North regarded a newspaper as a luxury for which people ought to be made to pay dearly. Lord Grenville considered that the press was the most powerful cause of the revolution in France. Burke and others feared that the press was an instrument of the subversion of morals, religion, order and human society itself. Windam insisted that newspapers circulated poison through the body politic every twenty-four hours. At Whig banquets, 'The Liberty of the Press' was a favourite toast; but when they returned to office in 1782, and again in 1806, the Whigs preserved the very same restrictions upon the press – like severe stamp duties and the buying of press support with laundered public money – operated by Tory governments. And, especially during the French Revolution and the unrest which persisted in the industrial districts after 1817, some tough-minded public figures, such as Southey, lost their nerve. They took advantage of a free press to fight the free press. They founded societies to crack down on the sale of 'democratic' literature. They even publicly justified flogging, hanging, transportation to the colonies and other drastic measures against activists in the popular grass-roots press for encouraging the 'inferior' orders to talk seditiously about their grievances.

Rethinking the classics

History is on every occasion the record of that which one age finds worthy of note in another.

Jakob Burckhardt, 1957

Not only was there a wide gap between the utopia of 'liberty of the press' and the reality of a limited-circulation, harassed and deeply corrupt press. The early European and American advocates of 'liberty of the press' also failed to see that their utopian vision contained several blindspots. We can leave aside until later in this essay the subsequent – twentieth-century – developments within the field of communications which were unanticipated by classical theories of press freedom. For the moment, let us look carefully at the *internal* problems of the classical theories. This should assist the project of developing a revised theory of freedom of communication capable of making sense of late twentieth-century media developments. At the very least, the effort to *rethink* the classical theories should cast doubts on the standard interpretation – Jürgen Habermas's *Strukturwandel der Öffentlichkeit* – which harbours a certain nostalgia for the heroic ideals of the early modern public sphere.[31]

To begin with, the advocates of a free press did not

---

[31] Habermas's intriguing call both to retrieve and to supersede the ideals of the 'bourgeois public sphere' has produced much criticism from his opponents. In some measure this has been justified, because the pathbreaking interpretation of *Struktur-wandel der Öffentlichkeit* never properly sketched an alternative

come to terms with the experience of *self*-censorship because they assumed that political power is the main 'external' threat confronting individuals who are otherwise 'naturally' capable of expressing their own opinions in public. The printing press – Marshall McLuhan's *The Gutenberg Galaxy: the Making of Typographic Man* (1962) reminds us – was the earliest example of mass production. Cheaply producible, multiple copies of printed material, from presses equipped with reusable, moveable typeface, revolutionized the world of publishing. It produced a flood of identical copies of texts in a way that vastly surpassed anything scribes could produce by hand. Yet the early modern press remained dogged by state censorship. Pre-publication policies of

---

model of the media and public life. That difficulty was compounded by three other weaknesses. First, *Strukturwandel der Öffentlichkeit* concentrated on *one* historical form of public life (that of the west European middle classes). This had the effect of making other, plebeian forms seem more repressed or insignificant variants of the 'bourgeois public sphere'. Second, Habermas's argument adhered too closely to the self-image of the early defenders of public life, with the result that it exaggerated its inner homogeneity and coherence. Third, Habermas's account of the 'refeudalization' of the public sphere drew too heavily on Adorno's melancholy theses on the mass culture industry. As a consequence, *Strukturwandel der Öffentlichkeit* failed to analyse the ways in which twentieth-century struggles to nurture public life can take advantage of new media developments. These weaknesses together produced within Habermas's argument a fundamental ambivalence. A nostalgia for the 'bourgeois public sphere' coexisted with a deep pessimism about the possibility of developing new forms of public life within civil society and the state. These points are developed in *Public Life and Late Capitalism*, chapters 2, 7, and acknowledged and discussed by Habermas in 'Vorwart zur Neuauflage 1990', *Strukturwandel der Öffentlichkeit* (Frankfurt am Main, 1990), pp. 11–50.

selective privilege were widespread. They involved the inspection of the contents of manuscripts and the rewarding of publishers who, in return for their coop-eration with the established authorities, enjoyed the advantages of a monopoly. After publication, authors, publishers and booksellers also had to reckon con-stantly with the 'book police'[32] and its apparatus of orders and methods of surveillance and petty harassments.

Under such pressures, it is understandable that the advocates of 'liberty of the press' typically thought of the censorship problem by means of the paradigm of negative liberty. The 'freedom of speech or of the press' (the famous phrase of the First Amendment) meant *negative freedom*, the freedom of individuals or groups of individuals to express themselves without prior external restraint, and subject only to government-enforced laws guaranteeing the same freedom equally to all other individuals. 'Liberty of the press' was thought of as an epic, heroic fight of the individual against political power, an heroic struggle in which the media of com-munication were viewed as a passive or neutral conduit through which information about the world circulates. This 'information-flow' paradigm failed to represent the ways in which the media of communication themselves pre-structure or 'bias' the reception of opinions by individuals located in space and time.[33] It mistakenly took for granted a world of facts or verities which have

---

[32] H. J. Martin, *Livre, pouvoirs et société a Paris au XVIIe siècle, 1598–1701* (Paris, 1909), vol. 1, pp. 442–3, 462–6; Daniel Roche, 'Censorship and the Publishing Industry', in Robert Darnton and Daniel Roche (eds), *Revolution in Print. The Press in France 1775–1800* (Berkeley, Cal., 1989), pp. 3–26.

[33] Harold A. Innis, *The Bias of Communication* (Toronto, 1951) and his 'Paper and the Printing Press', in *Empire and Communica-tions* (Toronto and Buffalo, 1972), pp. 141–70.

a determinable meaning and a world of (potential)
individual citizens who react rationally to these facts. It
failed to recognize that 'information' is itself structured
symbolically, that its 'codes' are subject continually to
acts of interpretation by individual citizens, who are
themselves in turn shaped by these same codes. Early
modern theories of liberty of the press lacked a language
in which they could reflect on the many and complex
ways in which modern media of communication engage
in story-building and story-telling activities guided by
stocks of recipe knowledge, institutional routines and
technical tricks. They relied upon unsophisticated
accounts of the complex process of producing, sending
and receiving information, in which communication is
sustained and produced by interpreting subjects acting
within contexts which are themselves structured by the
media of communication. In other words, the early
modern protagonists of a free press failed to recognize
that individuals are 'situated interpreters' and not all-
knowing subjects. They are always and everywhere
embedded in and constructed by communicative practices, such as the structures of the media, which set
agendas, constrain the contours of possible meanings,
and thereby shape what individuals think about, discuss
and do from day to day.

This misunderstanding of the recursive relationship
between 'individuals' and their media of communication explains why the early modern paradigm of 'liberty
of the press' had no clear grasp of the (quasi-conscious)
mechanisms by which individuals 'voluntarily' restrict
and confine their expressions. The twentieth-century
experience of totalitarianism has underscored the problem of self-censorship, which is certainly not restricted
to totalitarian regimes. Censorship, it turns out, is not

necessarily the all-seeing eye and iron fist of a distant authority which towers over its subjects. It is not only the experience, evoked in the opening chapter of Kafka's *Der Prozess*, of all those who have lived under modern despotism and who know the meaning of the early-morning knock at the door. Censorship can assume another form entirely. It can echo within us, take up residence within our selves, spying on us, a private amanuensis who reminds us never to go too far. The internal censor warns us that too much is at stake – our reputation, our families, our career, our jobs, legal action against our company. It makes us zip our lips, tremble and think twice, with a smile. It succours prevailing opinion and encourages 'the gramophone mind' (Orwell). Its hand even touches our children and friends, tutoring them in the art of not saying what they really think. Censorship resides in the lumpishness of our bodily gestures, in cautious and respectable clothing, and above all in intellectual cowardice, insipid humour, slothful imagination, and dissembled opinions wrapped in flat words.[34]

The early modern view of the relationship between liberty and the media also suffered from a hidden 'classical' bias. It extrapolated from the face-to-face model of communication of the Greek *polis*. It supposed that in complex, modern societies all citizens could enter public life on equal terms; that their freedom to express and publish their opinions would enable them to form

---

[34] The problem of self-censorship is discussed in George Orwell, 'The Freedom of the Press', *Times Literary Supplement*, 3680 (15 September 1972), pp. 1037–9; György Konrád, 'Censorship in Retreat', *Index on Censorship*, 2 (1983), pp. 10–15; and Miklós Haraszti, *The Velvet Prison. Artists Under State Socialism* (London, 1988).

themselves into a unified public body which would deliberate peacefully about matters of general concern.[35] Jacques Necker, whose *Compte rendu au roi* (1781) caused a sensation by publicly exposing, for the first time, the financial condition of the French monarchy, likened *opinion publique* to the highest law-giving tribunal, which filters and refines the inchoate opinions of the speaking, and listening public and submits its rulers to judgement, forcing them to act peacefully and in the open. Paine's discussion of the fundamental difference between liberty of the press and licentious uses of the press rests on the same classical assumption. While the press, according to Paine, should suffer no prior restraints by government, licentiousness should be defined not by government censors but by 'the public at large'. Kant's famous essay, *Beantwortung der Frage: Was ist Aufklärung?* (1783), is exemplary of this whole trend. It declares that 'the public use of one's own reason must be free at all times, and it alone can bring enlightenment to humanity', and it adds that 'the public use of one's own reason' means 'the use which each person makes of it as an expert before *the whole public of readers*'.[36]

The early modern assumption that communications media recreate the intimacy and directness of the *polis* neglected the problem of how freedom of communica-

---

[35] See Habermas, *Strukturwandel der Öffentlichkeit.*
[36] Jacques Necker, *Oeuvres complètes*, ed. A.-L. de Staël-Holstein (Paris, 1820–1), vol. 4, pp. 47, 50–1; Tom Paine, 'Liberty of the Press', in *The Life and Works of Thomas Paine*, ed. William M. Van der Weyde (New Rochelle, 1925), vol. x, pp. 287–90; and Immanuel Kant, 'Beantwortung der Frage: Was ist Aufklärung?', in *Schriften zur Anthropologie, Geschichtsphilosophie, Politik und Pädagogik* (Darmstadt, 1975), p. 55 (emphasis mine).

tion among citizens could be institutionalized peacefully in a dispersed, complex civil society. Advocates of 'liberty of the press' normally assumed that a free press could heal the wounds it inflicted upon the body politic. A free press implied the public airing and acceptance of divisions, factions, passions and conflicts. Yet these divisions were somehow to be healed by the rational and peaceful consensus generated by a free press. It was as if liberty of the press would ensure a politics without politics, as Peuchet made clear in his reflections on the eighteenth-century development of public opinion through a free press: 'It has extended the sphere of useful and beneficient principles, repressed a host of abuses, declared an implacable war against all the systems of persecution and intolerance; finally, it has become our firmest support for order, the guide and the guardian of *police* and of manners.'[37] Such expectations underestimated the practical difficulties of producing and distributing books, periodicals, newspapers and other publications to a mass reading public marked by different levels of literacy and wealth. In addition, they often failed to acknowledge that for reasons of time and geography not all citizens could simultaneously communicate their opinions or have access to the same sources of 'information'; in other words, that *differential* access to the means of communication is a necessary feature of modern civil societies. The homogeneous political community of the Greek *polis*, where citizens gathered together in public, spoke to each other directly, ruled and were ruled in turn, is impossible in the modern world, except sometimes in small groups and in

---

[37] Jacques Peuchet, 'Discours préliminaire', in *Encylopédie méthodique: Jurisprudence* (Paris, 1789), vol. 9, p. ix.

the momentary ecstasy of revolutionary situations.[38]

Most early modern defenders of liberty of the press correctly understood that citizens are free to the extent that they can exercise their capacities of continuous initiative in social and political life, and that such initiative requires unrestricted access to the means of communication of their opinions. James Madison's toughly worded original draft of the American First Amendment put the point emphatically: 'The People shall not be deprived or abridged of their Right to speak, to write, or to publish their Sentiments; and the Freedom of the Press, as one of the great Bulwarks of Liberty, shall be inviolable'[39] Such statements in defence of press freedom overlooked some elementary points about life as it was (and is today and will be tomorrow) in modern, complex societies. They somehow forgot that citizens cannot communicate by all speaking and writing and reading simultaneously (a rollicking farce could be written on attempts to do this); that, for reasons of technology and geography alone, not all citizens can be in the same place at the same time to communicate with their fellows; and that, in spite of its fundamental importance, liberty of communication is one of a great *diversity* of liberties, whose significance for different categories of citizens is inescapably variable and subject to continuous modification. In modern times, citizens tend to concentrate their energies in different ways and in various spheres of life. From time

---

[38] This is a theme of my *Democracy and Civil Society* (London and New York, 1988).

[39] 'Letter to Edmund Randolph (31 May 1789)', in *The Writings of James Madison*, Gaillard Hunt (ed.), vol. 5 (New York, 1904), p. 377.

to time, they also choose to alter their institutional loci of freedom. For all these reasons, simple conceptions of 'liberty of the press' need to be abandoned in favour of a more complex and differentiated notion of freedom of communication. The maximization of liberty of communication requires the enlargement of choices, which in turn requires both an increase in the variety of means of communication by which different groups of citizens *could* communicate, if and when they so wished, and the recognition that there are circumstances in which the freedom of expression of some citizens *conflicts* with the freedom of expression of other citizens.

In failing to grasp the nettles of complexity, the theory of 'liberty of the press' also left unacknowledged the key point that in large-scale societies *representative* mechanisms in the field of communications cannot be bypassed, so that some will necessarily communicate on behalf of others, if only for a time. 'In publicity consists the bond between a society and its goverment', re-marked Guizot,[40] failing to see that the media could never act as mere transmission belts of opinion, as if they were little more than innocent means of channelling information flows through the fields of social and political power. It would have been more accurate to draw analogies between a free press and the mechanisms of representative government. 'The representatives of a nation', Paul-Henri-Tiry, Baron d'Holbach, wrote in the *Encyclopédie* (1751–72), 'are elected citizens who in a limited government are charged by society to speak in its name, to stipulate its interests.' The early modern press functioned in a similar (if unelected) capacity. It

---

[40] M. Guizot, *History of the Origin of Representative Government in Europe* (London, 1861), p. 80.

was a means of re-presenting opinions: of rendering present opinions previously absent, without making them literally present, but only indirectly present, through an intermediary – the press itself.

Exactly because it served as an intermediary, the press was threatened permanently by the dangers of irresponsible or unaccountable communication. It is worth returning to d'Holbach: 'Experience shows us that in the countries that flatter themselves that they enjoy the greatest liberty, those who are charged with representing the people betray only too often their interests and deliver their constituents to the greed of those who wish to plunder them. A nation is right in distrusting such representatives and in limiting their powers.' Rarely did the early defenders of a free press bend this insight back on themselves. They overlooked the possibility that a free press rooted in civil society would constantly misrepresent its citizens. And they failed to broach the most basic controversy surrounding the meaning of representation: should representatives say and do what their constituents want? Are representatives obliged to act as if their citizens were acting for themselves? Or should representatives say and do what they consider best for their constituents? Are representatives only genuine representatives insofar as they interpret opinions, make judgements and act independently of their citizens?

The problem of how to render 'media representatives' accountable to their reading and listening publics normally went unrecognized in the writings of those in favour of a free press. The principal reason is that most proponents of 'liberty of the press' grafted their classical belief in the possibility of face-to-face communication on to a belief in the model of market-based media. The early modern ideal of a free press originated in the days of small-scale enterprise and widespread belief in decentralized market competition as a vital antidote to political despotism. It therefore should not be surprising that the ethos of market competition influenced the republican case for liberty of the press. Private property in the means of communication – the production and circulation of opinions through the process of commodity production and exchange – was typically seen as a key ingredient of freedom of communication. The market was viewed as an invisible, unbiased and gentle medium of circulating public opinions freely. It was regarded as an enclave of honesty, truth and integrity in a despotic world of secrecy, scheming and arrogance.

The intimate link between private property and liberty of expression was sometimes specified explicitly. An example is to be found in the famous and influential tract written by John Trenchard and Thomas Gordon, *Of Freedom of Speech* (1720): 'Without Freedom of Thought, there can be no such Thing as Wisdom; and no such Thing as publick Liberty, without Freedom of Speech; which is the Right of every Man, as far as by it he does not hurt or controul the Right of another; and this is the only Check which it ought to suffer, the only Bounds which it ought to know. This sacred Privilege is so essential to free Governments, that the Security of Property, and the Freedom of Speech, always go together; and in those wretched Countries where a Man cannot call his Tongue his own, he can scarce call any Thing else his own.'[40] This view was evidently too

---

[41] *Cato's Letters, or Essays on Liberty, Civil and Religious, And other important Subjects*, third corrected edition (London, 1733), vol. 1, p. 96.

sanguine about the capacity of market competition to
ensure the universal access of citizens to the media of
public communication. It failed to grasp the many ways
in which communications markets *restrict* liberty of the
press. It neglected to examine the inevitable tension
within markets between the free choices of investors
and property owners and the freedom of choice of
citizens receiving and sending information. In other
words, it failed to spot the difficulty of building a free
press, which required active, public-spirited traditions
of citizenship, on state-guaranteed market competition
which encourages individuals to see themselves as
private selves, as private property owners who stay
ahead of others by outcompeting them.

Precisely this tension became evident during the
eighteenth century. Market competition gave birth to
the first great press barons – to prominents such as
Charles-Joseph Panckoucke – who aimed to monopolize the opinion and reading market by producing truly
modern books, periodicals and newspapers.[42] Some
parts of the publishing industry, as the recent studies by
Gilles Feyel and René Moulinas show, became locked
into a complicated process of franchising and concentration of ownership.[43] Publishing was not a gentlemanly
game played according to the rules of honour. Some

---

[42] Suzanne Tucoo-Chala, *Charles-Joseph Panckoucke et la lib-
rairie française* (Paris, 1977).

[43] The case of the *Gazette de France*, France's first authorized
political newspaper, is analysed by Gilles Feyel, *La 'Gazette' en
province à travers ses réimpressions, 1631–1752* (Amsterdam and
Maarssen, 1982); the market pressures on publishing and book-
selling in the papal enclave of Avignon, which was unaffected
by French government regulations on printing and censorship
and therefore operated as a major exporter of counterfeit and
clandestine works, is examined in René Moulinas, *L'Imprimerie,
la libraire, et la presse à Avignon au XVIIIe siècle* (Grenoble, 1974).

parts of the publishing trade more closely resembled *brigandage*, a kind of 'booty capitalism' marked by scratching and scrambling in quest of the money and power brought by successful risk-taking in the market. Publishers were sometimes surrounded by pirates and spies and cut-throat rivals. For commercial reasons, they often suppressed public debate and political themes. The American colonial newspaper, for example, scrupulously avoided controversy up to the decade before the Revolution, when printers were dragged, against their will and commercial interests, into taking sides with the patriots or loyalists.[44] In order to stay in business, publishers were also sometimes forced to sell to the public whatever they could get away with, if need be through bribes, false advertising and counterfeit editions. They tried to capture the market by selling old texts in larger quantities and cheaper versions or by offering sensational new products. Publishers were often compelled to drop projects as fast as they could pick them up. And sometimes they were driven into bankruptcy by ferocious competition.

A final problem: the terms in which the ideal of 'liberty of the press' was defended and promoted by the critics of state censorship remained muddled, even self-contradictory in a philosophical sense. The subject of state interference with the press, as we have seen, excited a plethora of sophisticated philosophical arguments. These various justifications of liberty of the press certainly contain points of agreement. Each is critical of arcane and meddlesome state power. Each is biased in favour of civil society, regarding it as the proper site of

---

[44] Michael Schudson, 'Was There Ever a Public Sphere? If So, When? Reflections on the American Case', manuscript, Department of Communication, University of California, San Diego, December 1989.

the production and circulation of information among interacting individuals. Each banks on the market. Each places its hopes in the individual, whose potential for rational communication is hindered only by external impediments.

These points of agreement helped to bind together citizens who normally would not have seen eye to eye. 'Liberty of the press' became a volatile catchword among the opponents of despotism. It is nevertheless easy to see that the various justifications of liberty of the press are mutually conflicting in a philosophical sense. The criticism of state censorship in the name of the God-given faculty of reason enjoyed by certain individuals sits uncomfortably with the utilitarian principle of maximizing happiness by means of a free press; these arguments in turn do not sit squarely with either the consideration of freedom of the press as a 'natural right' or the defence of press freedom through the wholly secular and post-utilitarian idea that Truth is attained through unrestricted public discussion among educated citizens.

The evident philosophical incompatibility of these various justifications suggests a muddle in the self-understanding of early modern defenders of press freedom. This confusion was compounded by a fundamental self-contradiction within their defence of liberty of the press: the supporters of each theory sought to legitimate the unrestricted clash of opinions by presenting their own standpoint (God's will, the 'rights of man', the maximization of happiness, Truth) as unchallengeable. Freedom of communication was justified by reference to an absolute principle – less kindly, by falling back on the prejudice that there is one and only one right reason why liberty of the press is a basic, founding First Principle of social and political life. The natural-rights argument – to take just one example – rested on an essentialist picture of the self common not only to Enlightenment rationalism but also to Greek metaphysics and Christian theology: an ahistorical self which finds itself surrounded by inessential, contingent forces, events, things, whose meaning or significance is determined by this core self.

The key point is that the early modern theories remained insufficiently pluralist in a philosophical sense. They failed to apply their own suspicion of intolerance to themselves. They were instead underpinned by a quasi-secular version of the idea that the world is a divine creation, that it has an intrinsic nature which can ultimately be described, known, grasped and reshaped. A free press was assumed to be a vehicle for the spread of rational knowledge. When applied to contemporary institutions, such knowledge would expose and dissolve irrationality everywhere. It would aid the ordering of the everyday world – of bridges, machines, commerce and state constitutions – according to rational principles (God, natural rights, happiness, Truth) derived from experience itself. Held aloft by this assumption, defenders of liberty of the press very often viewed themselves as the agents of rational consensus. They considered intellectuals, broadly defined, as legislators capable of dissolving human irrationality, warding off uncertainty and piecing together the broken and fragmented viewpoints of the educated and articulate public.[45] 'Liberty of the press' suffered from the 'fetish of indivisibility' (François Furet). It was a weapon in the hands of the

---

[45] Zygmunt Bauman, *Legislators and Interpreters. On Modernity, Post-modernity and Intellectuals* (Cambridge, 1987).

know-alls in their struggle against the know-nothings. Defenders of liberty of the press thus trapped themselves in a performative contradiction. They sanctioned the open disputation of all except their own particular opinion on the nature of things. Like all idealogues, they tried to shield themselves against criticism by supposing themselves to be a universal language entitled to impose itself on the whole world. They assumed their ability to know everything, to refute their opponents and concretely to resolve all differences. This philosophical contradiction at the heart of the early modern case for press freedom today prompts some fundamental questions: can or should the principle of liberty of the press survive the collapse of the conflicting philosophical justifications provided for it by early modern writers? Can the principle be saved and reconstructed by stripping it of its incoherence? Or is the principle of liberty of the press salvageable only by admitting that it is a principle of *our* modern Euro-American civilization, which therefore should not seek to impose it on *other* civilizations?

Deregulation

The greatest danger to liberty today comes from ... the efficient expert administrators exclusively concerned with what they regard as the public good.

Friedrich Hayek, 1960

'If the early modern ideal of "liberty of the press" is seriously flawed, even on its own terms', a critic might ask, 'why bother discussing it three centuries after its birth? Why pay attention to a defective utopia from the past? Why try to reconstruct and intellectually spring-clean this classical utopia – to analyse it into its component parts and to reassemble it in a more plausible and appealing form?'

This essay offers a reply to these challenging questions. It argues that an appreciation of the strengths and weaknesses of the old discourse of 'liberty of the press' is today essential. It proposes that the attempt to recover and to reinterpret the early modern history of controversies and bitter conflicts about 'liberty of the press' is not an exercise in walking on air imported from the past. This is because in countries such as the United States, Italy, Poland, Germany and Britain a curious thing is happening. The old language of 'liberty of the press', shaped by the ethos of private market competition, is making a grand return to the centre stage of public debate about the future shape of the mass media. This language has forced a crisis in the prevailing (state-centred) understanding of the process of media representation. History appears to be repeating itself. The dead heroes in the early modern struggle for 'liberty of the press' are being brought back to life. Policy discussions about the press and particularly broadcasting are shaped increasingly by old-fashioned talk of state censorship, individual choice, deregulation, market competition and the dawning of an age of communications marked by 'freedom and choice, rather than regulation and scarcity' (Rupert Murdoch).

Murdoch is quoted here because his savaging of the principle of state-controlled media typifies this extraordinary revival of the old language of 'liberty of the press'.[46] Murdoch insists that market competition is the key condition of press and broadcasting freedom, understood as freedom from state inteference, as the right of individuals to communicate their opinions without external restrictions. Market-led media ensure competition. Competition lets individual consumers decide what they want to buy. It keeps prices low and quality high, forces suppliers to take risks and to innovate continually, lest they lose business to rivals offering better, improved products. A privately controlled press and a multi-channel broadcasting system in the hands of a diversity of owners is a bulwark of freedom. It is a permanent thorn in the side of the protagonists of cultural citadels and state tyranny. Market-led media liberate individuals from the dominance of state-backed, orthodox values. Competition ensures freedom of entry into opinion markets for any enterprise which thinks it has something individuals might like to hear, read or watch. Market-led media thereby cater to both mass and minority audiences, freeing them from the bureaucrats of television, radio and the press.

---

[46] Rupert Murdoch, 'Freedom in Broadcasting', MacTaggart Lecture, Edinburgh International Television Festival, Edinburgh, 25 August 1989, p. 4.

Not only media industry figures like Murdoch, but
market liberal intellectuals, politicians, government
policymakers and supporters of supra-national agreements such as the Treaty of Rome, have played a
decisive role in exhuming the bodies of Tom Paine and
other early modern protagonists of 'liberty of the press'.
Railing against state regulation, the market liberal body-
snatchers announce the dawning of an era of liberty for
all readers, listeners and viewers. Deregulation is the
idée fixe of the market liberal case. State-organized and
state-protected media, especially in the fields of broadcasting and telecommunications, are roundly con-
demned. They are said to be high-cost, inefficient and
ridden with restrictive practices. In the United States,
the vague licensing criterion stipulated by Congress –
the standard of 'public convenience, interest, or necessity' – is accused of distorting competition, raising barriers to entry and reducing service offerings. Certain
broadcasters, it is said, come to enjoy the permanent
fruits of 'bootstrapping', privileges granted by government which are then used to justify further government
support. The public suffers. In Britain, similarly, it is
said that the production and operating costs of the
BBC–ITV duopoly are excessive, due to a combination
of feather-bedding and cost-padding. This comfortable
duopoly is said to rest on oversized crews and an
oversized administration enjoying overpriced meals and
oversized expense accounts, which are guaranteed either
by a monopoly of tax finance upon households (the
BBC licence fee) or a monopoly of advertising finance
(as with ITV). The public service principle of universality – the principle that broadcasters should transmit
programmes that have wide appeal, cater for all tastes,
and offer to the whole nation access to the same number

of channels – is in reality a millstone around the necks of the principles of competition and choice in the media. State-protected media are also criticized for ignoring the interests of the advertising industry. It is argued that the media should simultaneously provide two services – supplying programmes to audiences and audiences to advertisers. Public service broadcasting fails miserably on the second count, according to some market liberals. The duopoly system in British broadcasting, for example, is criticized for restricting the number of 'commercial home minutes' or 'advertising messages' – the number of minutes devoted to advertising multiplied by the number of people listening or watching. In this way, the duopoly system, just like all monopolies which raise their prices by restricting their supplies of goods or services, milks business firms by imposing high direct costs on them in the form of monopoly rates for advertising. Some market liberals admit that certain propositions concerning the efficiency of competitive markets do not apply to the field of advertising. For example, they admit that there are no forces which can ensure that the price of television advertising is driven down to the costs of programmes. Consequently, advertiser-supported television is seen as an industry generating economic rents, that is, profits which exceed a reasonable rate of return and which are not eroded by competition. Nevertheless, the restriction of competitively priced advertising is generally seen to have undesirable consequences for both the economy as a whole and consumers of broadcasting in particular. Free markets in advertising bring about improved information. They stimulate product innovation, reduce prices and enhance competition among enterprises. To a certain extent market advertising also provides 'free' media, since advertising costs are not imposed directly upon newspaper readers or television viewers. Free markets in advertising guarantee audiences genuine choices of programmes and ensure that advertisers enjoy genuine competition in the purchase of airtime. Finally, market liberals attack the paternalism of state-protected media. According to them, the principle of public service broadcasting was corrupted from the beginning. In the United States, the trusteeship model of public regulation is accused of transforming regulators into 'super-citizens', charged with powers and obligations that go well beyond satisfying consumer demand. In Britain, it is said that the public service model was defined originally by nice young men sporting military moustaches and by prim officials with rolled umbrellas and black hats and speaking fraightfully good English. Contemporary public service has not shaken off these pompous prejudices. It rests unjustifiably upon nostalgic sneering at the ethics of business. It is based upon elitism, snobbery and anti-commercial prejudices: businessmen are portrayed as crooks; the upwardly mobile are shown as uncaring; money-making is despised. It supposes, further, that the whole nation can and should have access to the same number of channels, each offering programmes that have wide appeal and cater for all tastes. Public service media claim to be an instrument of the public good, not a means of handling people, entertaining them or of pandering to their passing wants. They are guided (in the words of the Italian Corte Costituzionale judgement number 59, 6 July 1960) by the principles of 'objectivity, impartiality, completeness and continuity for the country'.

In reality, public service broadcasting stifles the representation of individual needs and concerns. It squeezes,

confines and reduces choice. The programming decisions of public service bureaucracies are not subject to
continuing and detailed justification. These bureaucracies are involved in the continuous vetting of schedules
and programmes, and they exercise long-term power to
dissolve contracts which displease them. Public service
broadcasting involves systematic and arbitrary censorship of consumers' choices. The hand of government
is an unaccountable distributor of privileges and political favours. In the field of television, it is claimed,
government has always operated on 'the assumption
that the people could not be trusted to watch what they
wanted to watch, so that it had to be controlled by
like-minded people who knew what was good for us'.[47]
Public service broadcasting threatens liberty of expression. It tells us what is good for us. It flings us on to a
Procrustean bed of regulation. The BBC claim to
universalism, 'Others can inform some of the people all
of the time, or all of the people some of the time. Only
we can inform all of the people all of the time', is in fact
a mask for its own particular brand of paternalism. Its
real meaning was summarized more honestly by its first
General Manager, Lord Reith: 'It is occasionally indi-
cated to us that we are apparently setting out to give the
public what we think they need and not what they want
– but few know what they want, and very few what
they need.'[48]

So what is to be done about all this feather-bedding,
cost-padding, monopolistic advertising and paternalism

---

[47] Ibid., p. 2.
[48] Quoted in James Curran and Jean Seaton, *Power Without
Responsibility. The Press and Broadcasting in Britain* (London and
New York, 1988), p. 124.

of state-protected media? In the view of the marketeers, 'the perception of broadcasters as community trustees should be replaced by a view of broadcasters as marketplace participants.'[49] Monopolistic public regulation of the media is no longer justified. It is a species of socialism, whose time is up. Since socialism is seen as a temporary diversion on the road from capitalism to capitalism, the broad aim of policy in the media field should be to break the back of socialism by developing a system of market-based competition which provides readers, viewers and listeners with as many alternative sources of supply as possible, and thus treats them as sovereign, as the ultimate judges of their own interest. Whereas public service broadcasting involves the state in licensing favoured broadcasters and censoring from the air those whose values it does not share, markets allocate information resources by means of a competitive game. This game, like every game, may not always produce fair outcomes, but at least it is insulated against government control. The best antidote to the discretionary financing and arbitrary censorship of state-protected media is the impersonal and consumer-sensitive rationing system of market competition. In the field of communications, as elsewhere, the competitive market is the elixir of life. It is an unsurpassed mechanism for discovering, by trial and error, what consumers want, how these wants can be supplied at least cost, and whether new and challenging ideas and tastes will catch their eye.

In practice, this claim has radical consequences. Pub-

---

[49] Mark S. Fowler and Daniel L. Brenner, 'A Marketplace Approach to Broadcast Regulation', *Texas Law Review*, vol. 60, no. 207 (1982), p. 209.

lic service broadcasting must become leaner, more competitive and more efficient, and if it is to survive in the long term (market liberals are divided about whether it should survive) it must be reduced to the status of just one among many competitors for the citizen's dollar, lire, mark or pound. New televison and radio channels under private control are to be encouraged. Transmission facilities should be privatized gradually. Franchise contracts for independent companies should be put to competitive tender. Instead of government allocating frequencies to recipients who are chosen by a political process, spectrum assignments should be leased, sold or auctioned at the going market price. Existing licensees could be granted squatter's rights to their frequencies. After that initial grant, licensees and bidders would then be able to buy and sell broadcasting licensees freely.[50] According to many British market liberals, the BBC licence fee should be phased out and replaced by subscription. All restrictions upon pay-per-channel and pay-per-programme should be lifted, not only for cable but also for terrestrial and satellite operations. Encouragement should be given to the extension of cable and to multipoint video distribution systems (MVDS), which use microwave frequencies to deliver pictures. Subscription-based media of this type are said to be highly desirable because they provide greater choice, due to the direct contractual and monetary link between audiences and broadcasters. In general, a 'light touch' programming regime should be installed.

---

[50] Ibid., pp. 242ff. A classic defence of the allocation of spectrum through the market is R. H. Coase, 'The Federal Communications Commission', *Journal of Law and Economics*, 2 (1952), pp. 1–40.

There must also be a more comprehensive inclusion of advertising in broadcasting policy. Regulations that limit advertising and prescribe minimum amounts of non-entertainment programmes must be scrapped. Market liberals brush aside the conventional criticisms of advertising: that it stimulates expectations which it cannot satisfy; that it results from the wasteful rivalry between large firms; and that it creates barriers to entry, entrenches monopoly and, hence, inhibits market competition.[51] Advertising is not anti-competitive; it is profits which lead to higher advertising expenditure and not the other way round. Since it reduces other marketing costs and production costs (due to volume production), advertising also reduces prices, without any quantifiable deterioration in the quality of the service provided. Advertising is also considered an efficient method of providing 'free' television and radio. In any event, the fact is that advertising is already big business. For example, in Britain each year over £5.1 billion is spent on all forms of advertising, one-third of which is spent on television advertising. Annual expenditure on television advertising has been growing at an average rate of 5.6 per cent in real terms since 1970. In the United States, television advertising is most developed. Expressed as a proportion of GDP, television advertising in that country is 0.54 per cent, three times the average expenditure in western Europe and 40 per cent higher than in Britain. Many European market liberals argue for closing this gap. In their view a free and competitive advertising market is essential, since only it

---

[51] See, for example, Cento Veljanovski, 'Freedom in Broadcasting', *Institute of Economic Affairs Inquiry*, 1 (February, 1988), p. 7.

can ensure that the price of advertising is determined by demand, and not by the committee-driven decisions of bureaucrats.

In sum, market liberals insist that the media system must be encouraged or herded down the road of commodification. It must become more competitive and cost efficient. It must learn to love deregulation and, in the field of broadcasting, be forced to recognize that the old public service claim that there is insufficient radio spectrum to allow more television and radio channels has come unstuck. According to many free marketeers – and they are not alone in this belief – we are standing on the threshold of a technological revolution. This revolution in favour of technical plenty is as significant as the replacement of the handwritten manuscript by the printing press. The growth of new media, principally cable and low-power television, multipoint distribution service, cassettes, compact disc players and satellite broadcasting, and the convergence of broadcasting and telecommunications, renders the public service broadcasting model as vulnerable as a pedestrian huddled under an umbrella in a Scottish mist. The new technologies undermine the protected position of state broadcasting. Its privileges are said to date from the early twentieth century, when governments, treating broadcasting as an infant industry, sought to promote, not burden it. Broadcasting then was beset with technical problems. In the United States, for example, federal regulation of radio broadcasting emerged out of the 'etheric bedlam' and congestion in ship-to-shore communications. At that time, broadcasting was also a struggling business. Its future was highly uncertain. There was still considerable confusion about the nature of the electromagnetic spectrum, its potential uses, its divisibility and its capacity for development. Radio frequencies, free of congestive signal interference, were assumed to be in short supply. Companies first in the broadcasting business manoeuvred to secure government protection of their investments and their allocated frequencies. Politicians were anxious about their possible influence, listeners were a minority, and advertisers were ill-organized and unsure of the payoffs. A relative shortage of channels convinced governments to husband them for public use, but this in fact *created* a scarcity of spectrum. Licensees of channels were given every incentive to act as monopolists. The consequent shortage of spectrum then necessitated rationing schemes to allocate spectrum in non-market ways.

Many market liberals argue that the new information technologies blow such schemes and privileges sky-high. The new technologies make clear that scarcity is not an objective fact, and that policy, not physics, produces the shortage of frequencies. The new technologies make available sufficient spectrum for a dramatic increase in the number of channels. They thereby offer qualitatively greater consumer choice and, hence, the possibility of dissolving the familiar division between publishing and broadcasting by facilitating market competition in both spheres. An historical analogy with the field of publishing is often drawn. The abolition of public service monopolies would be a sign that broadcasting (and telecommunications) had finally come of age, just as the printing press and publishing did after several centuries of state regulation and censorship, which was finally broken by resistance from below by civil society. This time round, the breakup of public service monopolies *from above* would allow us at last to enter an age of full 'liberty of the press' encompassing not only books, periodicals and newspapers – the relatively primitive communications media of the early modern era – but more sophisticated electronic media such as television, radio and advanced telecommunications systems. Some market liberals emphasize the ways in which the advent of cable lifts limitations on spectrum.[52] Others speak of 'a global cornucopia of programming' (Murdoch) comprising nearly infinite libraries of data, educational material and entertainment, themselves linked by fibre-optic cable to telecomputers, all with a full capacity for interactivity. Still others (especially those attracted to technological determinism) anticipate a coming era in which 'the technologies of communication will serve to enlarge human freedom everywhere, to create inevitably a counsel of the people.'[53] All are agreed that market forces and 'advertising dollars', not 'megahertz',[54] are now the chief determinant of the amount of radio and television available to consumers.

---

[52] Ithiel de Sola Pool, *Technologies of Freedom* (Cambridge, Mass. and London, 1983), chapter 7.

[53] Leonard R. Sussman, 'The Information Revolution. Human Ideas and Electric Impulses', *Encounter*, vol. 73, no. 4 (November 1989), p. 60. The argument is developed in his *Power, the Press and the Technology of Freedom* (New York, 1989).

[54] Fowler and Brenner, 'A marketplace Approach to Broadcast Regulation', p. 223.

Market Failures

The idea of a self-adjusting market implied a stark utopia. Such an institution could not exist for any length of time without annihilating the human and natural substance of society.

Karl Polanyi, 1944

The opponents of market liberalism, particularly those who lean politically to the left, have been alarmed by these proposals – and justifiably so. Their criticisms are strongly emotive. The market liberal attack upon the feather-bedding, cost-padding, monopoly advertising and paternalism of state-protected media, they argue, is in reality a recipe for 'Americanizing' the media. It is a charter for advertisers and big business – for Murdoch, Mohn, Maxwell, Springer, Berlusconi, Lagardere and other giants of the media world. It endangers public service broadcasting. Critics point to the decadent effects of broadcasting deregulation in Italy, especially to the growth of such forms of '*TV spazzatura*' ('garbage telvision') as info-tainment (tasty court cases turned into pieces of baroque television) and glitzy striptease quiz shows. The point is reiterated at the EEC level by the critics of deregulation. They admit that the attempt to harmonize the media policies of member states and to create a unified European market (in accordance with the Treaty of Rome) will certainly swell market opportunities. But they insist that this will greatly increase the level of imported commercial productions, especially from American producers, whose competitive advantage stems from the economies of scale available in their unified domestic market and from the industrial processes of production and aggressive marketing developed by the American industry in response to that market.

In Britain, say other critics, reassuring words by the Conservative government about the BBC's special role as the cornerstone of British broadcasting are contradicted by the government's pro-market proposals. The BBC cornerstone is to be reduced in size. Its licence fee is to be phased out, some of its night hours assigned to commercial television and BBC radio prepared for privatization. The cornerstone is then to be crowbarred down the side road of subscription (which will clearly damage it in time, since most other channels except the BBC will be provided 'free' by advertising revenues). And the site on which the cornerstone once sat is to be filled with commercial broadcasting towerblocks and skyscrapers – additional satellite channels, a fifth television channel, the development of multi-channel local services through both cable and microwave transmission, and the replacement of the present ITV system by a regionally based Channel 3 subject to greater market competition. It is claimed that all this is likely to destroy public service broadcasting. The BBC model will be turned into a cultural ghetto. Quality will be thrown to the wolves of commercialism. Since multi-channel choice equals multi-channel drivel - cheap game shows, syndicated reruns and wall-to-wall entertainment programmes which resemble commercial advertisements – 'more choice' will mean worse, not better, media. It will mean broadcasting marked by low-cost productions and schedules built around repeats, long-running series and the extensive repackaging of existing materials. The foundation of excellence in the fields of public service radio and television will be wrecked. Public service broadcasting will cease to be the object of the world's envy and admiration. It will plummet to the level of tabloid newspapers.

This reaction, which to an extent is caricatured here, is justified. It nevertheless contains worrying gaps. Among the least obvious and most consequential is its secret dependence upon some worn-out clichés perpetrated by earlier twentieth-century theories of 'mass culture'. Conservative variants of the theory of mass culture – presented by Ernest van den Haag, T. S. Eliot, R. P. Blackmur and others – scorned the rise of mass culture as the work of rootless cosmopolitans skilled at using radio and other electronic media. Commercialized media were accused of undermining respect for traditional cultural authorities, eroding customary values centred on the family, religion and community, and manipulating and deceiving gullible flocks of passive consumers.

On the political left, the Adorno–Horkheimer theory of the culture industry proposed a strikingly parallel version of the latter part of this argument.[55] Late capitalist societies were seen to be caught blindly in the grip of commodity production and exchange. The world resembles a gold rush. The whole of life is structured by rules of equivalence, which forcibly compare, calculate and reify all commodities through the standardizing medium of money. The mass communications industry, Adorno and Horkheimer argued, reinforces such trends by destroying the distinction between high and low culture. It leaves behind a

---

[55] See Max Horkheimer and Theodor W. Adorno, *Dialektik der Aufklärung. Philosophische Fragmente* (Frankfurt, 1969), pp. 128–76; and A. Huet et al., *Capitalisme et Industrie culturelles* (Grenoble, 1977).

destructive trail of 'stylised barbarism'. The industrial-
ized news and entertainment from the culture industry
instruct, enchant and stupefy their customers. The
might of industrial capitalism is lodged in consumers'
minds. Real life becomes indistinguishable from the
reality presented by newspapers, movies and radio
programmes. The culture industry mass produces mass
deception, by encouraging individuals to identify with
the media in order to escape from everyday drudgery. It
makes them think that they are up to date with things,
that they know what is happening in the world, and that
they are successful and happy. Everybody is amused
into oblivion. Satisfaction expressed in clichés prevails,
pseudo-individualism becomes rife, and individuals are
encouraged not to think critically about anything. They
forget the suffering and injustice before their eyes. They
succumb to gold-rush fever.

The same fear of gold-rush fever agitates today's
intellectual critics of market liberalism, especially on the
political left. These critics emphasize the advantages of
preserving the old concern with the dangers of commercial mass media. Treading in the footsteps of Adorno
and Horkheimer, a critical 'political economy of mass
communication' (Garnham)[56] shifts attention from, say,
the Althusserian conception of the media as ideological
state apparatuses, which seems more suited to critical
analyses of state-controlled or public service media.[57]

[56] Nicholas Garnham, 'Contribution to a Political Economy of
Mass Communication', in his *Capitalism and Communication*
(London, 1990), pp. 20–55.
[57] Louis Althusser, 'Ideology and Ideological State Apparatuses (Notes Towards an Investigation)', in his *Lenin. Philosophy and Other Essays* (New York and London, 1971), pp. 127–
86.

Instead, it views the media as phenomena of civil society, that is, as primarily *economic* phenomena with both a direct role, through commodity production and exchange, as creators of surplus–value and an indirect role, through advertising, in generating surplus–value in other sectors of commodity production. This commodity-centred analysis correctly spots the profound significance of the market liberal defence of 'deregulation'. It grasps the possibility of a watershed in the contemporary revival of the power of market-based media, especially in Europe. It accurately senses that the era of public service broadcasting is coming to an end. Yet critical theories of the media which obscure the *self-paralysing tendencies* or *internal limits* of commodified systems of communication are inadequate. They fail to see that the production and distribution of opinion according to market criteria is possible only within narrow limits. Market-based media are not seamless and trouble-free. They cannot homogenize and pacify their audiences, nor can they fulfil their promise of 'freedom and choice, rather than regulation and scarcity'. Communications markets are self-paralysing. They regularly *create* endemic contradictions and dilemmas which belie their claims to openness, universality and accessibility.

This point about market failures requires closer examination. Market liberals emphasize that a genuine communications market requires, at a minimum, that consuming individuals can effectively and directly register their preferences, and that producers willing and able to finance their costs of production must have effective freedom of entry into the marketplace. According to two influential American market liberals, communications markets excel at 'promoting competition, removing artificial barriers to entry, preventing any one firm from controlling price or eliminating its competitors, and in general establishing conditions that allow the price of goods to be as close as possible to their cost of production'. Communications markets also ensure that 'consumer satisfaction is enhanced by freedom of choice in the price, quality, or variety of products.'[58] The trouble is that on both counts communications markets fail to live up to their own standards.

The arguments are less familiar than they might be. Unrestricted competition does not necessarily ensure freedom of entry of producers into the marketplace. Markets are often not contestable[59] because the levels of investment required to enter the market are too high or too risky, due to an existing stranglehold of monopolies or cartels that have already 'creamed off' the market potential. Markets are also sometimes not contestable because firms discover that the replication of production, transmission and distribution networks proves to be cost inefficient; that in practice it can even lead to destructive competition, whereby each competitor is drawn into a struggle resembling a fight between Kilkenny cats.

Such trends towards the concentration of media capital are evidently accelerated by market liberal policies. Sometimes 'deregulation' results in a form of cut-throat booty capitalism, of the kind unleashed by

---

[58] Fowler and Brenner, 'A Marketplace Approach to Broadcast Regulation', p. 210.

[59] W. J. Baumol, J. Panzar and R. D. Willig, *Contestable Markets and the Theory of Industry Structure* (New York, 1982). See also J. S. Vickers, 'Strategic Competition Amongst the Few – Some Recent developments in Oligopoly Theory', *Oxford Review of Economic Policy*, vol. 1, no. 3 (1985), pp. 39–62, and Robert Britt Horwitz, *The Irony of Regulatory Reform: The Deregulation of American Telecommunications* (New York, 1989).

the 'velvet revolutions' in central and eastern Europe.[60] At other times, the concentration process is less dramatic, as in Italy, where the slow breakdown of public service broadcasting since the mid-1970s has greatly increased the concentration of mass media ownership.[61]

---

[60] A cartoon in the East German communist daily, *Neues Deutschland*, shows a steamroller, its front wheel a massive roll of newsprint with the names of West Germany's four biggest publishers, bearing down on a tiny paper boat labelled 'Ost', in a puddle among the cobbles. 'We'll show you what we mean by press freedom', says the caption. This scenario was played out in Hungary in early 1990, when the German publishing giant Axel Springer Verlag AG took advantage of a legal loophole to gain control of four Hungarian newspapers without paying a pfennig. In the absence of Hungarian legislation on the disposal of state-owned assets, the corporation secured the agreement of the management to switch employers. Springer-Budapest's managing director, Jozsef Bayer, announced the takeover as follows: 'Hungary is in a judicial void. But when it comes to business, there is no power vacuum.' Such trends are not confined to newspaper publishing. Throughout the region, many communications media linked officially to the *ancien régime* are now seen as disreputable. Local capital for modernizing the communications infrastructure is scarce. Acute shortages of newsprint, publishing facilities and computers are chronic. Traditions of innovative and independent journalism are weak; many media workers are only familiar with the art of producing propaganda. The withdrawal of state subsidies has resulted in the collapse of many local (work-based and specialist) publications and the formation of a media vacuum. Booty capitalism thrives in these circumstances. Western media capital functions as 'a Pied Piper, encouraging publishers, broadcasters and policy makers to dance to the tune of money', (Vladimír Bystrov, Vice-President of the Syndikát Novinářů, interview, Prague, 20 October 1990).

[61] Guiseppe Rao, 'The Italian Mass Media and the Role of the Judicial System', manuscript, European University Institute and Università degli Studi di Firenze, Facoltà di Giurisprudenza, June 1990.

Although there are presently more than 4,200 private radio stations and 1,400 television stations there, deregulation has allowed the Berlusconi group to expand further its Fininvest empire. It comprises the ownership of the three main national private television channels (which strongly influence other networks by providing them with programmes, advertising and personnel), a lucrative film production company, two national newspapers, magazine publications, a radio network, the biggest Italian publishing company (Mondadori), and television channels in France, Germany and Spain. Fininvest also has interests in the insurance sector, the financial market and the real estate and construction sectors. It owns a national supermarket chain (Standa), about three hundred cinemas and a football team.

In Italy, as elsewhere, competition has eroded competition because it has forced media firms to protect themselves by becoming market leaders that stride leagues ahead of their would-be competitors. The concentration of media capital through competition is best documented in the world of newspaper publishing. The rules of Darwinian competition force publishers to gobble up their rivals – to expand in order to spread their bets and stabilize their revenues, and then to expand further to support the overheads generated by their original expansion. In post-war France, for example, this logic of concentration of press ownership and control through competition virtually destroyed the independent press which dominated newspaper publishing for several years after Liberation.[62] 'Market forces' created newspaper chains and press groups.

---

[62] J. W. Freiberg, *The French Press. Class, State, and Ideology* (New York, 1981).

Newspapers in small towns and cities went into decline, and independent press enterprises were forced into bankruptcy or bought out and absorbed. Aligned supply sectors (especially newsprint, printing equipment and newspaper distribution) were subject to monopoly pressures, and monopolistic advertising agencies patronized overtly depoliticized papers to the disadvantage of small, politically involved publications. The *engagé* political press was especially devastated: of the twenty-seven left, right and centre political papers of the Liberation period, only three survived until 1970.

Competition in the British newspaper industry has also eroded competition by forcing firms to protect their flanks by becoming market leaders. As James Curran and others have pointed out,[63] three men – Maxwell, Murdoch and Stevens – control 82 per cent of Sunday newspaper sales and 73 per cent of daily sales in Britain. During the post-1945 period, the press has become ever more tightly integrated into the core sectors of industrial and financial capital. Ownership of newspapers has become a key strategy by which large firms seek to outdo their competitors and to influence the market environment in which they operate. Rising costs and the redistribution of advertising have contributed to the near-decimation of the old social democratic press.

This general erosion of competition (contrary to the optimistic claims of many market liberals) has not been reversed by the introduction of computerized page make-up and plate-making techniques, facsimile machines, new web-offset machines and other new

---

[63] James Curran, 'The Press in the Age of Conglomerates', in Curran and Seaton, *Power Without Responsibility*, chapter 7.

production technologies. Entry costs are high and rising in the newspaper business. The establishment fund of *The Independent* was £21 million, reinforced by further credits of £3 million; £22.5 million was invested initially in *Today* and *Sunday Today*; and Robert Maxwell's *The European* was launched on a tight budget of £25 million. This is an international growth pattern. Everywhere the trend is towards cross-media ownership on a global scale, with Rupert Murdoch's News Corporation as the exemplar of this process of conglomeration. The Murdoch holdings sprawl over four continents, and include vast assets spread equally across magazines, newspapers, books, films and television. The empire includes magazines such as *New York*, *New Woman*, *Seventeen* and *TV Guide*, itself the largest circulation (17.1 million) magazine in the United States. Murdoch's company controls nearly two-thirds of metropolitan newspaper circulation in Australia and one-third of the national distribution in Britain. Although the company built itself primarily on racy tabloids, it also publishes more 'upmarket' newspapers like *The Times* and the *Sunday Times*, the *Australian* and the *Boston Herald*, and co-publishes the *Financial Times* and the *South China Morning Post*. Murdoch has interests in ten book publishers, including HarperCollins. Murdoch's Sky Channel, a satellite broadcasting service for cable-television viewers, claims to reach more than 13 million households in twenty-two countries. In the United States, the company has used its ownership of Twentieth Century Fox film studios and six independent television stations to launch the Fox Television Network, which produces tabloid-style television programmes like *A Current Affair* (which specializes in prime-time baby-sitter horror stories, extramarital romps and mystery deaths),

The Simpsons and *DEA*. It also controls a large film library, including such blockbusters as *Aliens* and *Cocoon* and the syndication rights to popular shows like *M⋆A⋆S⋆H* and *L.A. LAW*. Its 108-channel Sky Cable, providing satellite-to-home television services in the United States and Canada, is planned for 1993.

The Murdoch empire, in which everything is English-language related, has been created by buying indigenous communications systems and linking them globally. Assets total US$13 billion. In 1987, News Corporation earned US$560 million on revenues totalling US$3.5 billion. The company's current debt exceeds US$4.7 billion, and annual interest payments exceed US$600 million. Despite this, Murdoch runs the giant corporation like a family firm. He was among the first to recognize that media companies, which are traditionally cash rich and asset poor, have been undervalued in market terms. This has allowed him and his relatives to own half the shares, most of their acquisitions being financed by borrowing and through the sale of assets.

The market liberal fetish of 'the market' not only plays down its monopolistic tendencies. It is also contradicted by evidence that high risks and high entry costs sometimes discourage all potential producers wanting to enter communications markets. Markets are not only uncontestable but sometimes *abandoned* by all (potential) investors. As Keynes pointed out in *The Means to Prosperity* (1933) and in the twelfth chapter of *The General Theory of Employment, Interest and Money* (1936), market competition tends to generate uncertainty and 'holding back' among investors. The propensity of firms to invest in the communications field always depends upon expectations about likely market conditions in the future. These firms will normally find it impossible to provide fully credible guarantees of future conditions, and they may, as a consequence, be unwilling to invest their capital. Or, coy and hard to please, they may invest cautiously, with inegalitarian consequences. An example: if the unit cost of providing telephone services to isolated rural areas is much higher than in urban areas, and if the objective of firms is to minimize risks and maximize profits, then unless firms are absolutely certain that rural subscribers are prepared to pay qualitatively higher costs than their urban counterparts – a certainty the firms do not have, since they suffer from 'imperfect information' – they may well be unwilling, due to 'market forces', to supply rural users with new or equivalent telephone services.

The 'crises of confidence which afflict the economic life of the modern world' (Keynes)[64] result from the deep uncertainty and lack of foresight generated by 'free markets'. A case in point is the unwillingness of capitalist investors to enter into new ventures involving videotex service. This technology has been available in some countries – as Prestel in Britain, Telidon in Canada, and Bildschirmtext in the Federal Republic of Germany – only on a rather user-unfriendly and closed-user-group basis because no private investors, advertisers or governments have been willing to shoulder the risks associated with its introduction for wider public use. Because of the comparatively low rates of return on the huge infrastructural investments required, private capital invests elsewhere. Or it waits for state intervention, which in effect draws in tax payers to carry the cost of the distribution system. Meanwhile, private

---

[64] J. M. Keynes, *The General Theory of Employment, Interest and Money* (London and New York, 1960), p. 161.

firms take the profits from the sale of hardware and from the subsequent development of markets in such consumer durables as teletex decoders.

In France, by contrast, a graphics-based videotex service, Teletel/Minitel, was made widely available for the first time in the world through active support from the DGT, the French government telecommunications agency.[65] Initially, terminals were provided free to the public in an attempt to make it a service for not only businesses and professionals, but also residential users and other citizens. Minitel now contains around 12,400 service codes. It is accessed cheaply (on a monthly rental and pay-per-use basis) and easily via the public telephone system, and enables users to search a telephone directory, reserve a train ticket, teleshop, bank money, learn a foreign language, receive news and send mail, or arrange a rendezvous. The service has difficulties, including the fact that there is no itemized billing for accessing particular services (thus producing complaints, for instance by parents about high bills incurred by their children). The service is also underused by the least wealthy and powerful groups of citizens (such as blue-collar workers, retirees, the new underclass) at whom it was expressly targeted. Within firms, Minitel is also sometimes used by management, under the rubric of 'improved communication', the better to control their employees. Despite such difficulties, the proponents of the system have been successful in creating huge numbers of *minitelistes* (more than five million terminals have been installed throughout France). This success underscores the continuing importance of *non-*

---

[65] The following details are drawn from a seminar delivered by Alain Briole, Trinity College, Dublin, Eire, 26 June 1990.

market or decommodified mechanisms in developing a public communications system by reducing the entry costs for users and producers, thereby overcoming the deficient and inequitable provision that chronically affects market competition. The market liberal claim that the market maximizes individual freedom of choice is also doubtful. Unrestrained market competition in fact tends to work strongly against the choices of certain citizens, especially of minorities and temporary or floating majorities. Radio and television broadcasters, for instance, know that when they compete for audiences the best way to maximize their audience share is to jostle for the heartland of viewers by offering mass appeal programmes. This leads to insufficient diversity in programming and wasteful duplication of programme types. The overall programme fare becomes relatively thinner, more repetitious and more predictable than would otherwise be the case. Inevitably, the ratings dominate. But ratings under-represent the opinions of ethnic and regional minorities, gays and lesbians, greens, elderly citizens, socialists and other minorities.

Ratings also discrimate against non-market forms of television aimed at children.[66] On the three principal commercial networks in the United States, for instance, schedules during early weekday mornings, after-school hours and Saturday mornings are stuffed full of programmes like *Smurf's Adventures*, *Fraggle Rock*, *Bugs Bunny and Buddies*, *The Flintstones*, *Dennis the Menace* and

---

[66] Edward L. Palmer, *Television and America's Children: A Crisis of Neglect* (New York, 1988); and Tom Engelhardt, 'The Shortcake Strategy', in Todd Gitlin (ed.), *Watching Television* (New York, 1986), pp. 68–110.

Teenage Mutant Ninja Turtles. Robots and Smurfs, muscular blonde princes and fruit-scented princesses, furry bears and anti-terrorist squads come and go. They push and shove each other off the screen every half an hour or so voicing lame homilies (what the industry calls 'prosocial messages') such as 'Don't fight', 'Watch out for smooth-talking strangers', 'Be happy', 'Be a good student'. These figures also participate as licensed characters on a stage of product advertising and promotional tie-ins; they are commodities linked to board games, comic books, toys, cereals, home videos and other commodities marketed by a multi-billion dollar industry. Thanks to 'deregulation' of children's policy guidelines in the early 1980s, children's programmes on the three networks often resemble programme-length commercials. Since the demise of *Captain Kangaroo* in the early 1980s, regular weekday educational programming for children has become rare. Commercial television not only does not provide an adequate variety of educational and informational programming for children as a whole. It also fails for the same reason to satisfy the principle that the most stimulating and effective educational messages are those tailored to specific age groups (for example, 2–4 year olds, 9–11 year olds) rather than to vague masses of children in general. The reason is that commercial television operates in a system of rewards based primarily on audience size. Since children have less purchasing power in the marketplace than adults, they are of little interest to advertisers, except as an amorphous assemblage of consumers. The basic procedural rule of commercial television is quietly but surely ageist: shows should not be sold to viewers, but viewers must be marketed to advertisers.

This under-representation of particular audiences is unwittingly revealed in Hayek's metaphor of the wearing away of a footpath across a field.[67] The pathway, as Hayek notes, may well be the unplanned product of a multitude of individual choices. But to say, as Hayek does, that the result eases the journey of everyone in the present and future is to overlook the fact that some individuals are not used to travelling Indian file. They find the path ill-suited to their needs, unsuited to bicycles, inconvenient or too indirect, or untraversable because they walk poorly or not at all. The under-representation of particlar audiences is a fundamental flaw in market-led media, especially considering that we all belong to these and other minorities some of the time, while some belong to a minority all of the time. Ratings also fail to measure the intensity of citizens' media preferences. Audience research suggests, for example, that although the social profile of viewers of current affairs programmes and *Dallas* fans may be quite similar, the former are considerably fewer in number and more spirited and enthusiastic supporters of 'their' programme. Under conditions of open market competition guided by ratings, current affairs viewers would almost certainly find their programme either withdrawn or relocated to a midnight or Sunday morning slot. They would be forced to recognize that a major problem with market competition is that it ensures that some win and others lose.

Unrestrained market competition works against citizens' choices in yet another way. Their participation

---

[67] The pathway example is developed in Friedrich Hayek, 'Scientism and the Study of Society', in his *The Counter-Revolution of Science* (Glencoe, Ill., 1952), chapter 4.

in the marketplace of communications costs money, which some either do not have or cannot afford to spend. Freedom of the press, A. J. Liebling once quipped, is limited to those who own one in the marketplace. Most market liberals normally gloss over this problem with blithe references to 'the increasing prosperity and greater leisure time and expenditure' of audiences.[68] Their more sophisticated friends explain that a market-based multi-channel delivery system of communications may increase – not reduce – the communicative abilities of the less advantaged members of civil society. In a free communications market, 'relatively impoverished interests' can buy modest slices of space or time. This trend is said to be well-established in publishing. Although entry into print publishing requires skill and much capital, buying space in an established publication costs much less.[69]

Such claims overlook the fact that in the field of communications, as elsewhere, market competition picks the pockets of the poor. Effective demand, the willingness and ability to pay for access to opinions transmitted through the media, constantly overpowers actual and potential demand which is not backed by resources of time, money and know-how. Market competition produces a growing division between the (relatively) information rich and the information poor. Citizens with stable employment and high disposable income (often serviced by their own corporate or professional organizations) can better afford and better

---

[68] *Broadcasting in the 90s: Competition, Choice and Quality. The Government's Plans for Broadcasting Legislation* (London, 1988), p. 5.
[69] De Sola Pool, *Technologies of Freedom*, pp. 142–3.

access space and time in the media. They can also better access new communications gadgets, products and services – sophisticated peritelevision sockets capable of interfacing with a decoder to process encrypted signals; personal computers equipped with a modem; portable fax machines; camcorders; satellite conferencing facilities; satellite-linked mobile telephones; listening typewriters; and high-definition supertelevisions. Meanwhile, other citizens, particularly those who find themselves trapped in the new underclass now rapidly developing throughout western and central-eastern Europe and the United States, are forced deeper into debt (after hire-purchasing a satellite dish or high-definition television). Or they are relegated to using second-rate communications media: to cut-price pay television, advertising-funded, cheaply produced radio and television, an ailing postal system and the telephone three streets away that half the time seems to be out of order.

These patterns of unevenly distributed choice generated by commodified media are exacerbated when market competition is oiled by advertising. Advertising encourages a general shift away from diversity of coverage towards the packaging of 'product lines' into 'light entertainment'. Advertising stimulates the growth of pseudo-newspapers, such as *Bild am Sonntag* and *The National Enquirer*, and fuels the circulation of magazines and journals which are stuffed with ads and then given away free of charge in underground stations and shopping malls or pushed through the mailboxes of suburban homes. In the field of television the same trend is evident. Advertising commercializes the structure and content of programmes. Certain programmes (such as *Amazing Discoveries*) become indistinguishable from

advertisements. Advertising transforms programmes
into its own valets. Since the success of any programme
is measured in terms of advertising revenue and audience size, there is little space for radical experimentation
and little time in which to allow off-beat programmes
or performers (such as the *Monty Python* group) to 'find'
their audience. (In the United States, oft-cited exceptions such as CBS's *The Waltons*, which survived poor
early ratings only because of a sustained write-in campaign, prove this rule.) It is as if schedules are drawn up
and programmes produced solely to highlight advertising. There is no time to develop anything in depth. To
attract the attention of the audience, and to make room
for the next clump of advertisements, points must be
developed fast. Shot length must be reduced. Sound
bites are forced to become exceptionally short. Dramatic narratives are hollowed out. Unrestricted advertising
encourages the growth of the type of fast-moving,
cheaply produced programming ('satellite slush') evident on Super Channel, with its bland *mélange* of Dutch
football, world golf sponsored by Korean Air, re-run
ads for Kelloggs cereals and Clausthaler beer, third-rate
Australian movies, *Flipper* and other old Hollywood
standbys, ice hockey, American college football and
corporate-sponsored news and weather in slow, tedious
English.

The key point is that those who pay the piper always
want to call the tune. Media advertising is not a
guarantor of freedom of choice. 'Advertising men shoot
where the ducks are thickest' (Andrew Neil),[70] and that
is why advertising actually restricts the listening, reading and viewing choices of at least some citizens – a

---

[70] *The Late Show*, BBC (20 November 1989).

tendency (as the Peacock Committee in Britain and the German Federal Constitutional Court have both recognized)[71] which holds over a wide range of estimates for the price and income elasticity of demand for advertising. Advertising works in favour of advertisers and businesses and against citizens. It privileges *corporate speech*. Bent on maximizing audiences and minimizing costs, advertising ensures that material which is of interest to only a small number of citizens will at best be available on a limited scale. Advertising reduces the supply of 'minority interest' programmes, aesthetically and intellectually challenging themes, and politically controversial material which fails to achieve top audiences and, hence, does not entice advertisers to upon their chequebooks.

The trend in favour of corporate speech is strongest in the United States, where communications media have been subject during the past three decades to a virtual takeover by the corporate voice.[72] In that country, the marketeers' case for the rights of corporate speech resonates in a culture which remains under the spell of early modern individualism, of the kind which fuelled arguments for 'liberty of the press'. Speech is often regarded as an individual exercise – as natural as the family doctor, the small farm or intrepid self-made individual entrepreneur. It is ironic that this prejudice has strengthened the constitutional hand of large cor-

---

[71] *Report of the Committee on Financing the BBC* (London, 1986); *Decisions of the Federal Constitutional Court*, vol. 73, pp. 118 and 155ff.

[72] See Warren Freedman, *Freedom of Speech on Private Property* (Westport, Conn., 1988); and Herbert Schiller, *Culture Inc.* (New York, 1990).

porations, who have taken advantage of the First Amendment, which turns a blind eye to corporate power by prohibiting only the federal and state *governments* from abridging free speech. The language of individualism is used to crush individualism. The free-speaking individual is replaced by corporate actors wielding enormous power in the field of information – the giant among self-promoting giants being Time Warner, an US$18 billion conglomerate, whose media concerns include specialized television channels, millions of cable subscribers, dozens of national magazines, book publishing and a large proportion of global song recordings. These concerns are so vast that Time Warner, having commissioned one of its journalists to write a novel, could then publish the book and market it through a Time Warner book club, review it in Time Warner magazines, and make it into a Time Warner movie, which in turn could be the source of further reviews and interviews and feature stories before being broadcast on Time Warner cable television.[73]

This trend is sometimes exaggerated by its critics, who warn of the 'systematic envelopment of human consciousness by corporate speech'.[74] Following Adorno and Horkheimer, they condemn advertising for

---

[73] Ben H. Bagdikian, 'The Lords of the Global Village', *The Nation* (12 June 1989), pp. 805–20.

[74] Schiller, *Culture Inc.*, p. 45; cf. Wolfgang Fritz Haug, *Critique of Commodity Aesthetics* (Cambridge, 1986), which attempts to 'derive the phenomena of commodity aesthetics from their economic basis' (p. 8), and which concludes that advertising is a capitalist confidence trick; 'by serving people, in order to ensure their service (to capital), it brings an unending stream of desires into the open . . . it can offer only an illusory satisfaction which does not feed but causes hunger' (p. 56).

universalizing false images of abundance, novelty and freedom of choice. In reality, say its critics, corporate advertising encourages individuals to fling themselves onto the treadmill of commodity consumption. Workers are transformed into consumers, who produce in order to consume. Women, who are the principal targets of advertising, are encouraged to believe that shopping is their work and way of life. Advertising also promotes social ladder-climbing; it makes respectable the Club Méditerranée culture of the *nouveau riche*, promotes the narcissism of the poolside and nourishes the smiling anonymity of the supermarket. Advertising deadens the nerves of civil society. It seduces citizens into using and discarding some things and into disregarding others. Private desires stifle public spirit: nobody cares a nickel about anybody but themselves. Profanity, mindlessness, glitz and waste triumph. In sum, advertising not only encourages individuals to wallow in commodities which they actually do not need. It also 'manufactures a product of its own: the consumer, perpetually unsatisfied, restless, anxious, and bored. Advertising serves not so much to advertise products as to promote consumption as a way of life.'[75]

There is some truth in these claims. Advertising does indeed promote the consumption of specific products and encourage the spread of a 'consumer way of life'. It stimulates the growth of a three-minute culture studded

---

[75] Christopher Lasch, *The Culture of Narcissism* (New York, 1978), p. 72; cf. the argument of Dallas Smythe that the central function of the mass media is not to sell packages of ideology to consumers but to manufacture and sell audiences to advertisers, in 'Communication: Blind Spot of Western Marxism', *Canadian Journal of Political and Social Theory*, vol. 1, no. 3 (1977), pp. 3–21.

with visual slogans and sound bites signifying almost nothing: 'A lot more Chevette for a lot less money'; 'Coke is it'; and 'Save more – have less to buy later!' Advertisers sometimes tell stories riddled with sexist, homophobic, nationalist, racist or other ideological assumptions; advertising promotes commodities with potentially harmful ecological effects; and it regularly exploits individuals' anxieties and fails to satisfy the hopes and dreams which it stimulates.[76] Yet stern critics of advertising – as well as its devotees in the advertising and marketing professions – typically understate the difficulty of measuring the effects of advertising as well as overstate the degree to which its force-fields magnetize adult audiences.[77] Compared with adult audiences riveted to sports prorammes, feature films, sitcoms and talk-back radio, those confronted with advertisements are much more fidgety, bored and distracted. During commercial breaks, they prefer to make tea, pour a drink, reach into the refrigerator, do housework or channel hop. Advertisements are widely understood as 'propaganda'. Only a tiny minority of audiences can recall advertisements they have already seen or heard. This is not because they are cultural dopes with deficient memories: most of the time, most adult individuals do not perceive themselves to be in the market for the products being advertised. Even when they are, commercials very often 'mis-hit' or 'overshoot' their target. Commercials regularly mis-communicate because the actual audiences they address are quite different in

---

[76] Fred Hirsch, *Social Limits to Growth* (London, 1976).

[77] See Michael Schudson, *Advertising. The Uneasy Persuasion* (New York, 1984); and William Leiss, Stephen Kline and Sut Jhally, *Social Communication in Advertising: Persons, Products and Images of Well-being* (Toronto, 1986), especially part 3.

disposition from the hypothesized or targeted audience. For these various reasons, advertising regularly fails to secure 'consumption as a way of life' by manipulating the hearts, minds and taste buds of consumers. Corporate advertisers tacitly acknowledge this. Despite their saturation of newspapers, magazines, radio and television with commercials, businesses rarely invest large proportions of their annual budgets in advertising; in their overall business plans, they rarely pin their hopes on the supposed persuasiveness of advertising. They do not operate on the assumption that they are ventriloquists capable of speaking through consumers of the utility of products, the better to sustain market exchanges. Advertising–funded media nevertheless remain incompatible with freedom of communication among a plurality of citizens. Advertising tends to edge out from the public domain, silently and by stealth, *non-commercial* opinions and *non-market* forms of life. A good case can certainly be made in the abstract for advertising as a legitimate means of publicizing information about the prices and the current and future availability of goods and services. It is also important not to conflate commercial advertising with its other forms. A regulated system of political advertisements, granting all serious contestants for governmental office a fair chance to communicate their views to voters, arguably assists the free circulation of opinions so necessary for a democracy.[78] And there is evidence that advertising is a

---

[78] See Margaret Scammell, 'Political Advertising and the Broadcasting Revolution', *The Political Quarterly*, vol. 61, no. 2 (April–June 1990), pp. 200–13; and Kathleen Jamieson, 'The Evolution of Political Advertising in America', in L. L. Kaid et al. (eds), *New Perspectives on Political Advertising* (Champaign, Ill., 1986).

versatile and sophisticated form of social communication. It provides the symbolic tools for the circulation and disputation of everyday meanings, some of them unintended by advertisers. Advertising is among the most important vehicles for 'presenting, suggesting and reflecting an unending series of possible comparative judgements'.[79]

Yet in practice *corporate* advertising has a nasty habit of rating itself too highly, of striving to entomb its targeted audiences in a pyramid of commercial speech. The main trouble with corporate advertising is that it fosters the undemocratic assumption that a consumer way of life is *the* life. Its significance is thus not confined to specific advertisements or to particular product categories or brands. Advertising peddles the assumption that the consumption of marketed goods is the key sign of social identity. Advertising is in this sense an ideology, a *grand récit* (Lyotard). It is a particular form of (potentially) hegemonic language game which functions, not always successfully, to mask the conditions of its own engendering as well as to stifle the pluralism of language games within the established civil society in which it thrives. Advertising is a scavenger. It attempts, unjustifiably, to annex and feed upon every other *particular* language game by representing itself as a general or universal language game, as unquestionable, and as therefore freed from the contingencies of historical time.[80]

The overall point to be made about the market liberal fetish of market competition is this: the time has long passed when it could be assumed credibly that market

---

[79] Leiss et al., *Social Communication in Advertising*, p. 247.
[80] This revised meaning of the concept of ideology is elaborated in my *Democracy and Civil Society*, pp. 213–45.

competition guarantees freedom of communication. The old ideal of 'liberty of the press', brought back to life by the market liberals, is redolent of a time of hand-set pamphlets, penny newspapers, limited edition moral and scientific treatises, and widespread belief in decentralized market competition as the chief antidote to political despotism. Since those days, the patterns of ownership and control within the private sector of publishing, radio and television have become highly integrated, oligopolistic and bureaucratic. Multi-media enterprises, operating transnationally and communicating messages which are shaped and driven by market economic imperatives, are the prevailing model of development in the private information sector. This trend urgently needs to be publicized since, historically, the proponents of 'liberty of the press' directed their criticisms mainly against the *state* regulation of market-based communications media. Today, by contrast, friends of the 'liberty of the press' must recognize that *communications markets restrict freedom of communication* by generating barriers to entry, monopoly and restrictions upon choice, and by shifting the prevailing definition of information from that of a public good to that of a privately appropriable commodity. In short, it must be concluded that there is a structural contradiction between freedom of communication and unlimited freedom of the market, and that the market liberal ideology of freedom of individual choice in the marketplace of opinions is in fact a justification of the privileging of corporate speech and of giving more choice to investors than to citizens. It is an apology for the power of king-sized business to organize and determine and therefore to *censor* individuals' choices concerning what they listen to or read and watch.

Market liberalism insulates itself against this conclusion because it conceives of 'censorship' too narrowly, as the exercise of the monopoly power of the *state* to curb the exchange of opinions among various groups of citizens. Market liberalism interprets 'liberty of the press' as the outcome of a long and heroic struggle of private entrepreneurs to free themselves from duties and restrictions that either government or 'the public' may seek to impose. It envisions an exclusive estate, appropriating to 'the media' strong and favourable advantages over all others who do not belong to this estate. State interference with its operations is seen either as unjustified or as a necessary evil, for instance, in emergency conditions when the sovereignty of the state is threatened, or when (as in controversies about pornography or racism) certain citizens call on the state to prosecute other citizens for libel or slander or 'indecent' expression. The problem is that market liberalism misses the point that markets are complex structures within which corporate decision makers routinely act as censors. Market competition produces market censorship.[81] Private ownership of the media produces private caprice. Those who control the market sphere of producing and distributing information determine, prior to publication, what products (such as books, magazines, newspapers, television programmes, computer software) will be mass produced and, thus, which opinions officially gain entry into the 'marketplace of opinions'.

In times of crisis, this market censorship tends to

---

[81] Sue Curry Jansen, *Censorship: The Knot that Binds Power and Knowledge* (New York and Oxford, 1988), and 'Market Censorship and New Information Technologies', paper presented at the Polytechnic of Central London, 26 November 1988.

become overt. Restraint and 'objectivity' give way to open polemic and bitter campaigns against 'enemies' of the market. In normal times, the processes of market censorship are less visible and more subtle. Censorship of this type is not an underhanded conspiracy to swindle or brainwash gullible publics for the sake of profit and to 'reproduce capitalist relations of production'. It results rather from the fact that commercial publishers of opinion are little interested in the *non-market* preferences of readers, listeners and viewers. They are instead primarily concerned to satisfy the demands of audiences within the boundaries of market competition. Media entrepreneurs certainly provide choices, but they are always within the framework of *commercially viable* alternatives. Corporations operate on the assumption that market competition is the substructure and that citizens' choices are superstructural. Individuals are treated as market-led consumers, not as active citizens with rights and obligations. Audiences and readers are not offered the choice, for instance, of participating as citizens in decisions which shape the overall investment and marketing strategy of the firm. They are not asked whether they wish to alter their patterns of consumption by cutting back on unsustainable patterns of economic growth. The market liberal talk of 'freedom and choice, rather than regulation and scarcity', when decoded into plain English, means exactly this: 'We assume that a market-based capitalist economy is here forever. It is legitimate and viable, indeed the best system ever invented for satisfying individuals' demands. We offer you all kinds of choices so long as you, the consumer, restrict your choices to the terms agreeable to us, the entrepreneur. If you don't agree – well, tough. Why not start up your own company?'

The Democratic Leviathan

Every sovereign, centralized state is potentially aggressive and dictatorial.

Simone Weil, 1933

The market liberal case for press and broadcasting freedom is not only spoiled by its fetish of market competition. It is often further discredited by its affection for the unaccountable and arcane power of state institutions. Modern states, remarked Robert Southey in the early nineteenth century, can no more stand without pens than without bayonets.[82] This maxim might well have been phrased as a long-term prognosis, for all Western democracies are today faced by a gathering problem: the long-term drift, largely unplanned, towards a loose community of interlocking states, whose undemocratic structures of decision making are multi-layered, quasi-supra-national and equipped with various mechanisms for powerfully regulating and distorting the exchange of information and opinion among their citizens. The symptoms of this long-term trend are already quite evident. The flow of opinion among citizens is hindered by the executive use of old-fashioned prerogative powers and new techniques of official information management. It is obstructed by the resort to secrecy and dissimulation and the recurrent appeal to the principle of the sovereignty of the state

---

[82] Quoted by William Jerdan in *Men I Have Known* (London, 1866), p. 413.

('national security'). And, since the First World War, the cause of political censorship has been furthered by the steady spread of unsupervised corporatist mechanisms and by 'invisible' forms of local, national and supra-national government – departments, commissions, agencies and intergovernmental conferences which normally are neither accountable to citizens or their mass media, nor subject to the rule of law.

It is curious that neither the marketeers nor their critics pay much attention to these trends, despite their profoundly disturbing implications for our understanding of democracy. Unaccountable power has always been regarded as scandalous in democratic countries, and yet those countries are now faced by a permanent scandal. The core of all democratic regimes today contains the seeds of despotism. The historic (if never completed) transformation of early modern absolutist states into late modern constitutional states governed by parliaments is over. We are entering a new era of political censorship, the age of the democratic Leviathan, in which key parts of life are structured by unaccountable political institutions equipped – as Southey might have observed – with old and new pens of various shapes and sizes.

A revised theory of 'liberty of the press' must come to terms with these forms of state interference in the process of publicly defining and circulating opinions. Five interlocking types of political censorship warrant particular attention. They are described as ideal types and examined below in order of their familiarity:

(1) *Emergency powers*. Time-honoured attempts by governments to bully parts of the media into submitting

directly to their wishes by means of instructions, threats, bans and arrests continue to make their presence felt in Western democracies. Such techniques of political repression come in two forms. *Prior restraint* (as it was known originally in constitutional circles in the United States) includes all those informal and formal procedures – from the friendly chat and cocktails with a government spokesperson and simple requests or warnings delivered by telephone to the issuing of mandatory and discretionary guidelines – whereby the publication of matter (be it oral, visual or print) is vetted by the state authorities. *Post-publication censorship* operates from the time of the initial publication of material to its dissemination. It may include legal action taken against material already available in civil society. It normally leads to the banning, shredding, burning, reclassification or confiscation of books or visual material (photographs or paintings, films or videos), or the confiscation of the technical means by which that material has been produced. Post-publication censorship may also extend to the closure of newspapers, printing houses, radio and television stations. It may encompass the banning of particular 'anti-state' organizations and the censoring and punishing of journalists for 'condoning terrorism' by expressing their sympathies for such organizations.

Especially in times of (alleged) crisis, these two sub-types of political repression of the media are often combined. The media are seen by the political authorities to have no useful or legitimate function unless as accessories to the armoury of the state. The media come to play a distinctive political role. They ensure that a latent crisis becomes manifest by rendering collective the feeling of crisis among citizens, and by amplifying the claim of state officials that drastic action is required to remedy the crisis, which they have defined as such through the media.

The direct muzzling of the media by the French government during its war against Algeria is a sobering (and by no means exceptional) case in point.[83] During the transition from the Fourth to the Fifth Republic, amidst mounting public tension and fears of an army takeover spearheaded by General de Gaulle, the press was routinely threatened, censored and seized. Editors were notified by the government that 'France' was in danger. Ministers briefed journalists about precisely what could and could not be reported, insisting that such briefings were strictly confidential. Direct bans were imposed on certain kinds of information, such as news of house arrests, expulsions and the use of anti-guerilla tactics. In Algeria itself, *L'Express*, *Libération* and *L'Humanité* were banned totally for various lengths of time. Most liberal and left papers were seized numerous times in metropolitan France. Since seizure amounted to blocking the distribution of a publication *after* it was printed, even if a censored article were replaced, the entire print run had to be repeated, leading to a doubling of costs of production. Newspaper publishers were subject to extensive bombing campaigns by 'unidentified attackers', and journalists were arrested and convicted on charges of disclosing military secrets and 'attacking the morale of the army'.

(2) *Armed secrecy*. Modern state power thrives upon police and military organs which are shrouded in secrecy. The reason is obvious: there is no better way in

---

[83] Claude Bellanger et al., *Histoire générale de la presse française* (Paris, 1976), especially pp. 166, 173.

which state officials can outmanoeuvre their domestic or foreign opponents than to learn about them by monitoring their activities, without being monitored in turn. This dynamic underpinning the growth of invisible 'repressive state apparatuses' is certainly evident in twentieth-century Western democracies. Police and military apparatuses marked by secrecy, cunning and the insistence on compulsory unanimity within the organization are normal features of democratic states. They are also deeply antithetical to political democracy and to freedom of communication.

The problem of armed secrecy, Kant and others observed, was evident within the operations of early modern governments, which appreciated, for example, the value of planting informers in opposition groups at times of crisis. Wars and revolutions were typical breeding grounds of armed secrecy.[84] Yet until the late nineteenth century these systems of shadowy armed power were improvised and transient, being built around the capabilities of specific groups of officers and linked to individual government ministers and particular threats or sudden crises. Or (as in America) secretive armed power remained in private hands; the surreptitious gathering of information about social groups was conducted by private policing agencies, such as the union-bashing Pinkertons, who hired themselves out to businesses and other organizations of civil society. All this changed in the early years of this century. Between the summer of 1909 and the autumn of 1911 in Britain – whose permanent institutions of armed secrecy were among the first to develop – MI5 and MI6 were born

---

[84] See Friedrich Meinecke, *Machiavellism: The Doctrine of Raison d'Etat and its Place in Modern History* (New Haven, 1957).

and the modern Official Secrets Act was passed. The 'D-Notice' system for vetting newspaper stories bearing on 'national security' was devised. A register of aliens living in Britain was established, blanket interceptions of certain categories of mail at the Post Office began, and the Special Branch was transformed into a domestic counter-subversion agency.[85]

After this time, the bureaucratic instinct for survival ensured the permanence of secret police and secretive military organizations within the state. Their continuity was guaranteed less by dangers to the state and more by budgetary allocations and such mundane concerns as offices, desks, telephones, files and pension plans. This trend in Western democracies was greatly strengthened by the onset of the Cold War, and by attempts to portray domestic dissent as linked to dangerous international enemies. This has resulted in a well-organized form of permanent political censorship at the heart of state power. Governments regularly control official press releases and authorize briefings in matters of 'national security'. Information is classified or reclassified as 'secret'. Public documents are weeded. Dirty tricks are covered up. Selected citizens have their phones tapped, their homes bugged and offices broken into without the benefit of a judicial warrant. Government officials in the intelligence, military and police are subjected to a duty of 'lifetime' confidentiality.

The growth of armed secrecy has recently produced bizarre effects. Parts of the elected executive branch of the state have snooped on their potential rivals and

---

[85] Bernard Porter, *Plots and Paranoia: A History of Political Espionage in Britain 1790–1988* (London, 1989); cf. Gary T. Marx, *Undercover. Police Surveillance in America* (Berkeley, Cal., 1988).

disinformed legislatures systematically (the Watergate affair).[86] The police have conducted clandestine paramilitary operations against either their peaceful opponents (the *Rainbow Warrior* bombing)[87] or their violent enemies (as in the bombing campaigns and assassinations in Spain conducted by the shadowy Anti-terrorist Liberation Groups, or GAL, whose function was to terrorize Basque terrorists and their sympathizers).[88] Extensive junta-like operations (such as the Iran–Contra affair) have been conducted behind the backs of elected authorities.[89] And state paramilitary secrecy has been used to protect secretive anti-state organizations employing paramilitary tactics (the Piazza Fontana massacre and the Gladio affair).[90] Finally, the phenomenon of secret armed power has spread into the realm of intergovernmental negotiations. The routine conduct of NATO and WEU affairs, for example, involves the integration of national defence bureaucracies with transnational defence organizations; these in turn create centres of power which escape the control of any single member state, government or Parliament. Supranational military organizations shift decision-making power away from legislatures. They increase the level of

---

[86] Jeffrey C. Alexander, *Watergate and the Discourse of Civil Society* (forthcoming).

[87] John Dyson, *Sink the Rainbow! An Enquiry into the 'Greenpeace Affair'* (London, 1986).

[88] Melchor Miralles and Ricardo Argues, *Amedo: El Estado Contra ETA* (Barcelona, 1989).

[89] Theodor Draper, 'Reagan's Junta', *The New York Review of Books* (29 January 1987), pp. 5–14.

[90] Norberto Bobbio, 'Democracy and Invisible Power', in *The Future of Democracy* (Cambridge, 1987), pp. 79–97 and his interview, 'Nessuno può più tacere', *Il Manifesto* (2 November 1990), p. 7.

electoral unaccountability and secrecy of government operations. And, since the growth of supra-national organs encourages particular governments to allege the necessity of political compromise with other governments, it leads governments everywhere to formulate 'flexible' negotiating positions, thereby discouraging legislatures from 'interfering' in supra-national negotiations.

(3) *Lying*. The nasty business of lying in politics is a characteristic feature of democratic (and other) regimes. The belief of politicians that half of politics is image-making and the other half the art of making people believe the imagery, whatever 'the facts', is rampant; the old maxim that politicians can be understood only by watching their feet and not their mouths remains true. The practice of lying is partly an inheritance from the early modern period. During the phase of state-building and the formation of nation-state politics, truthfulness was rarely counted among the political virtues. Kant's insistence that lying is never justified, never even to save a friend from probable murder – a thesis he directed against Benjamin Constant during the Thermidorean phase of the French Revolution[91] – is a cry in the wilderness of modern political power. Outright lies and calculated secrecy, as Hugo de Grotius pointed out in *De jure belli ac pacis* (1625), were always regarded as legitimate means of achieving political ends.

In recent decades the commitment to the 'methods of

---

[91] Immanuel Kant, 'Über ein vermeintes Recht, aus Menschenliebe zu lügen', *Kant's Gesammelte Schriften*, vol. 8 (Berlin, 1912), pp. 423–30, a reply to Benjamin Constant, 'Des réactions politiques' (1797), in *Ecrits et discours politiques*, ed. O. Pozzo di Borgo (Paris, 1964), pp. 21–85.

defactualization' (Arendt) has assumed two new forms. The art of political lying has adopted the tough charm, parrying 'good will' and slick-tongued tactics of the Madison Avenue public relations person. This is the art practised by numerous government press officers: throwing critics off the trail, calming nerves, keeping journalists happy, preparing stories for public consumption with a careful eye to making them credible. This art of lying through public relations is most fully developed in the United States, where White House staff regularly seek to shape the media's portrayal of the president. Administration is viewed as a continuous public relations effort. Statements from various government departments are vetted and tightly coordinated. Press conferences are used to project the opinions of the presidency. Certain reporters are accredited; questions are planted; follow-up questions are disallowed; 'cream puff' topics are given priority; and, since Truman, carefully prepared opening statements help set the agenda for reporters in attendance. The administration provides a range of 'services' to the media, such as interviews, photo opportunities, background sessions, travel accommodations and daily handouts. Briefings are especially important occasions for gentle lying. Briefings may be 'off the record' (the information reporters receive may not be used in a story); 'on the record' (remarks may be attributed to the speaker); 'on backround' (a specific source cannot be identified although general descriptions of its position and status – such as a 'White House source' – are permitted); or they may be 'deep background' (in which case no attribution is allowed). When these (potentially) mendacious methods fail, the administration attempts to punish the media for coverage perceived as unfair, unfavourable or both. Particular journalists are asked to choose between their career interests and their critical opinions of the government. In extreme cases, media hostile to the administration are denied access to official sources.[92]

The art of political lying has also wrapped itself in the technocratic methods of professional problem-solvers. The routine lying which proliferated throughout the civilian and military branches of the American state during the Vietnam War – the 'progress reports' tendered to Washington by subalterns mindful of their career prospects, the doctored bombing reports and the phony body counts of the 'search-and-destroy' missions[93] – was of this kind. This technocratic form of lying feeds upon models and hypothetical scenarios. It locks itself into its own house of assumptions, shutting all doors and covering all windows. It has an aversion to common sense and a strong dislike of the accidental. It reckons judgements to be primitive and favours sophisticated calculations. It finds strength in think-tanks, advisers, formulae and marathon information campaigns. And it speaks a pseudo-scientific language that unifies and apparently makes sense of the most disparate situations, events and personalities.

(4) *State advertising.* The rulers of the early modern state, especially during its absolutist phase, regarded

---

[92] In the American context, this trend is examined by George C. Edwards III, *The Public Presidency. The Pursuit of Popular Support* (New York, 1983); and Michael Grossman and Martha Kumar, *Portraying the President: The White House and the Media* (Baltimore, 1981).

[93] See Daniel Ellsberg, 'The Quagmire Myth and the Stalemate Machine', *Public Policy* (Spring, 1971), pp. 262–3; and Ralph Stavins et al., *Washington Plans an Aggressive War* (New York, 1971), pp. 185–7.

themselves as the source and principle of unity in a particularistic society of orders and estates. These executives of state power sought to protect and legitimate themselves by taking counsel from others – through parliaments, individual and corporate petitions, personal networks of informants – and by peddling their own opinions among the clients of state power. Southey's remark about bayonets and pens drew attention to this latter mechanism. In Europe, the *London Gazette*, which first appeared under the title of the *Oxford Gazette* in 1665, was among the most famous and influential of these organs of government advertising.[94] It channelled officially sanctioned interpretations of foreign news: 'What came in the foreign mails is in the *Gazette*' was a constantly recurring phrase. Its single folio sheet reported the sovereign's speeches to Parliament, and found space for royal proclamations and resolutions of the Privy Council. Promotions at court were also reported to the public: to be 'gazetted' is still the formula of career advancement. In addition, the *Gazette* printed information provided by informers, published the numbers of winning tickets in government lotteries, and made space available for those advertisements for bear grease for baldness and other quack remedies which were so prominent a feature of eighteenth-century journalism.

Today, the methods of the *London Gazette* have become more sophisticated and a regular feature of all Western democratic governments. Government advertising is big and serious business. The self-promotion of state power absorbs a budget of nearly £200 million a year in Britain – where the state is the second largest

[94] Laurence Hanson, *Government and the Press 1695–1763* (London, 1936), chapter 4.

advertiser, behind only Unilever – covering 'campaigns' on every conceivable policy matter. The steady growth of state advertising gives all democratically elected governments enormous power of blackmail. Since most independent newspapers, radio and television stations rely heavily on revenue from advertising for their survival, threats by governments to withdraw such funding tends to produce compliance with pressures or even the collapse of such ventures. The growing ability of governments to use parts of the mass media strengthens this trend (and reinforces the patterns of lying through public relations work, mentioned above). Media reporting based on unattributed backdoor leaks, and the authorized and informal briefings of the 'lobby system', are well-known examples. Other examples include government campaign advertising (backed by professional consultants, actors, actresses, film directors and hiring agencies),[95] official press releases and kite-flying – the unacknowledged spreading of rumours or disinformation by governments to test the currents of public opinion. The official accreditation of experts with pro-government views also serves to legitimate (or increase the level of visibility of) official sources, thereby coat-tailing the media to the management of opinion by governments.[96]

The positively slanted coverage of political leaders through television and radio interviews is a less obvious but no less important example of state advertising. In recent years, intimate links have developed between broadcasting journalists, with their firm views of what

[95] Larry J. Sabato, *The Rise of Political Consultants* (New York, 1981).

[96] Edward S. Herman and Gerry O'Sullivan, *The 'Terrorism' Industry: The Experts and Institutions that Shape Our View of Terror* (New York, 1990).

the audience has the right as citizens to know about the actions of government, and the executive, backed by phalanxes of government information agents, press officers and other minders arguing almost legalistically with producers about the rules of engagement and appearance. Political interviews tend to become vehicles for political persuasion and veiled party-political broadcasts. The outward form of the journalistic interview is preserved, but the story is framed by the ground rules (concerning transmission duration, the timing of an interview, and the importance of having 'the last word') laid down by the interviewees. Questions designed to make politicians answerable to publics are replaced by questions intended to please politicians and to let them say what they like. Journalists climb into the pockets of politicians. Government statements become 'noble lies'. This trend is summarized by a leading British broadcaster: 'As television has become a medium of marketing more than of broadcasting, so the advertising cast of mind manifest by government has caught journalists by surprise. In the past press officers have wanted to channel and control the journalists' understanding of the story. Today, they see us as another outlet, more volatile but not dissimilar to an advertising slot. A newspaper can talk to a politician and there is no supposition that every word uttered will be reported. On television, there are demands for effective control of the editing. It is as if the appearance belongs to the interviewee.[97]

---

[97] Quoted by the managing director of the BBC World Service, John Tusa, in his 'Marketing Politics on TV', the *Independent* (17 May 1989), p. 21; cf. J. Heritage, 'Analysing News Interviews: Aspects of the Production of Talk for an Overhearing Audience', in T. van Dijk (ed.), *Handbook of Discourse Analysis* (London, 1983).

(5) *Corporatism.* During the twentieth century, networks of private sector organizations performing functions for the government through the devices of negotiations, grants and contracts have become commonplace. A substantial number of decisions of public consequence are taken, not by executives, or in legislatures or markets, but in bargains struck between the 'representatives' of social groups, or between these groups of civil society and the state itself.[98]

Corporatist procedures of this kind have resulted from the offloading by the state of a considerable number of its functions to the non-state organizations of civil society, whose key power groups have demanded a share of political power. Consequently, the boundaries of state and civil society intertwine. They are mediated by the bargaining, jostling and shifting compromises of 'public' officials and state machinery and private, 'non-state' agencies. Corporatism is a process of state intervention which contracts out official status to interest groups and organizations, who are charged to a greater or lesser degree with the formulation and/or implementation of public policy. Corporatism brings strategically important functional groups inside the state – 'politicizing' parts of civil society – while at the same time extending the state sphere into civil society, thereby 'socializing' certain state functions. This process is

---

[98] P. Schmitter and G. Lehmbruch (eds), *Trends Towards Corporatist Intermediation* (London, 1979); Claus Offe, *Disorganized Capitalism. Contemporary Transformations of Work and Politics*, ed. John Keane (Cambridge, 1985), chapter 8; and T. Modeen and A. Rosas (eds), *Indirect Public Administration in Fourteen Countries* (Abo, 1988).

patterned and tiered in complex and dynamic ways. It operates at different levels of decision making,[99] and appears to broaden the general franchise by supplementing territorial forms of political representation with functional modes of decision making. Trade unions, businesses, professional associations and other organizations become integral and indispensable components of public policymaking because they have a monopoly of information relevant for government. They also often exercise a substantial measure of control over their respective constituencies. But none of this guarantees the 'openness' or 'representativeness' of corporatist procedures. They tend to be highly elitist. Government personnel are not directly subject to parliamentary election or control. The 'private' bargaining organizations are also structured bureaucratically: their negotiators tend to instrumentalize the rank and file membership, who are relegated to the role of policy-takers, and to define agendas from the viewpoint of the corporate body. The costs of decisions are passed off onto the less powerful and more poorly organized groups of civil society.

Corporatist procedures have also developed behind a veil of confidentiality and extra-legality. Although permanent features of the political landscape, such procedures are rarely given legal form and not often

---

[99] The distinction between macro-/meso- and micro-corporatist procedures is developed in A. Cawson (ed.), *Organised Interests and the State: Studies in Meso-Corporatism* (London, 1985); G. Lehmbruch and P. Schmitter (eds), *Patterns of Corporatist Policy Making* (London, 1982); and W. Streeck and P. Schmitter (eds), *Private Interest Government* (London, 1985).

subjected to the requirements of public accountability. They constitute a form of government by moonlight.[100] Corporatist procedures are not obliged publicly to reveal, to explain and to justify their activities. Decision makers are under no *ex ante* legal obligations to consult widely on the range of choices available to them. Nor are they subject to *post hoc* obligations, for example, to justify publicly either their patterns of expenditure or the degree of success or failure in achieving the goals which they have set themselves.

These five interlocking trends in Western democracies are worrying. They indicate the growing quantity of political power which is normally unaccountable either to citizens or to the mass media, or not subject to the rule of law. If the rule of law (A. V. Dicey's phrase)[101] means the systematic elimination of arbitrary state power from political life, where arbitrary power is power immune from public evaluation and criticism, and insensitive to and incapable of learning from its environment, then without exaggeration we can speak of a growing lawlessness in Western democracies.

In Britain, the home of parliamentary democracy, lawlessness is rife and, to make matters worse, legalized state censorship of opinion and even state censorship of what has been censored is spreading. The list of symptoms of this trend is alarmingly long, and growing. Ministerial and administrative power is virtually immune from judicial scrutiny. Parliament exercises little

---

[100] Patrick Birkinshaw et al., *Government by Moonlight. The Hybrid Parts of the State* (London, 1990).

[101] A. V. Dicey, *Introduction to the Study of the Law of the Constitution* (London, 1885).

more than a marginal control over policymaking and implementation. Semi-governmental bodies (quangos), local authorities and departments enact regulations of all kinds, but there is no general requirement that these decisions respond to outside suggestions. Whenever advice is given and sought, it is normally an *ex parte* matter. Citizens have no way of knowing whether or not officials have been unduly influenced by private interested parties, and they have no rights even to know the rationale of officials' final decisions.

This state of lawlessness has been greatly supplemented by various government clampdowns. During the 1980s, the Thatcher governments sought to protect official secrecy and to patch up a culture of prudent silence and mumbo-jumbo within public institutions by charging outspoken civil servants (Sarah Tisdall and Clive Ponting).[102] During the battle for the Malvinas, it conducted an 'information war'. The instinctive secrecy of the military and the Civil Service were reinforced; public opinion was manipulated through lies and misinformation, and sections of the press were encouraged to connive with the government's own distortions.[103] The government made a failed attempt to suppress *Spycatcher*, the memoirs of the former MI5 officer Peter Wright. Prime Minister Thatcher toughened the Prevention of Terrorism Act, arguing that democracies 'must find ways to starve the terrorists and hijackers of the oxygen of publicity on

---

[102] See David Caute, *The Espionage of the Saints. Two Essays on Silence and the State* (London, 1986), pp. 99–212.
[103] See the account of Robert Harris, *Gotcha! The Media, the Government and the Falklands Crisis* (London, 1983).

which they depend'.[104] There was overt censorship of radio plays, news and documentaries on BBC and ITV: the Foreign Secretary sought to prevent a documentary exploring the SAS shooting of IRA members in Gibraltar in 1988, and proposals for ensuring the 'impartiality' of drama documentaries and other programming were circulated. Journalists employed by the *Guardian, Independent, Observer, Mail on Sunday* and *Sunday Times* were intimidated – and prosecuted – for articles on matters ranging from insider dealing to international terrorism. Bizarre legislation opposing the publication by government of material likely to 'promote homosexuality' was introduced. And the revised Official Secrets Act (1990) imposed an absolute, lifelong vow of silence on members and former members of the security and intelligence services; uniquely in criminal law, a person could thus be convicted without the opportunity of mounting any defence. The Act extended the blanket ban on disclosures of information to any other state official or journalist who is notified by the government that she or he is covered by it. In matters of defence and international relations the Act made it a criminal offence to make a 'damaging disclosure'. A disclosure is deemed

---

[104] 'Thatcher Urges the Press to Help "Starve" Terrorists', *New York Times* (16 July 1985), p. A3. The Prevention of Terrorism Act includes provisions that force citizens to report to authorities all contacts with members of the Irish Republican Army and the Irish National Liberation Front or their supporters, and to provide information that may be useful in government efforts against them. Failure to comply with the provision can result in criminal prosecution. The Thatcher governments specifically interpreted the provision to include interviews by journalists, which makes interviews more difficult and dangerous for journalists and proscribed organizations.

damaging if it harms 'the capability' of any part of the armed forces, or 'endangers the interests of the United Kingdom abroad' or 'seriously obstructs the promotion or protection' of those interests – or if it 'would be likely to' have any of those effects.

In all this there is a striking paradox: many market liberals love to talk of the need for a free communications market without censorship, and yet at the same time they are defensive of these trends and unsympathetic or hostile to citizens' attempts to extend the rule of law, to reduce the arbitrariness and secrecy of political power.[105] Their market 'libertarianism' coexists with a deeply neo-conservative attachment to political and cultural authoritarianism. The market liberal vision of a free market in communications is seen to require a powerful, authoritative state which acts as an overlord of the market. The sinews of a 'free' society, it is

---

[105] The Thatcher governments' views were typical. In a letter (dated 26 May 1989) to the British initiative for radical constitutional reform, Charter 88, whose founding document I co-drafted, Prime Minister Thatcher summarized her tough-minded views on the current state of civil and political liberties in her country: 'The Government considers that our present constitutional arrangements continue to serve us well and that the citizen in this country enjoys the greatest degree of liberty that is compatible with the rights of others and the vital interests of the State. The Government could not consider any constitutional reforms which were not widely understood and supported in Parliament and in the country at large. Furthermore, the Government does not feel that a written constitution in itself changes or guarantees anything: everything depends on how constitutional guarantees, whether written or unwritten, are interpreted and applied in daily life. Some of the more oppressive states in the world have written constitutions. Yours sincerely, Margaret Thatcher.'

claimed, are provided by coherent administrative power, by the bold, decisive action of statesmanlike politicians, and by governments' willingness to enforce national traditions and the laws of the land – against the internal and external enemies of the state and the market.

In this respect, market liberalism succours the old doctrine of sovereignty of the state. This doctrine originally had no meaning at all apart from the system of absolute monarchy in which it was born. According to the various theories of sovereignty of early modern writers such as Bodin, Althusius and Hobbes, the people are a body crying out for a head. This head is ultimately indivisible and absolute. Especially in times of public calamity and (threatened) crises of the body politic, it has the exclusive right to silence its subjects and to speak on their behalf. The sovereign is an earthly god whose power resembles that of the master who issues commands to his slave, or the father who disciplines his children. Guided by the principle *salus rei publicae suprema lex* (the safety of the state is the supreme law), the sovereign, whether by divine right, natural law or the fact of conquest, is duty-bound to govern as cunningly as possible. Sovereignty requires the *arcana imperii*, that is, it feeds upon the mysteries and aura of state power. It is constantly on the look-out for enemies at home and abroad. It must perforce be a form of rule which is both secretive and deceptive. Arcane dealings and noisy and pompous displays of power are the two sides of the sovereign state coin. Those who rule must not only *dissimulate* their power, which is most effective when they know and see without being seen by their subjects. Subjects must not only know that there are some who watch over them without knowing the location of the watchtower; they must also live in awe of the magnificence of the state. Sovereign state power requires *simulation*, visible signs of its supremacy: escorts of soldiers, splendid clothing, sparkling crowns and sceptres, elaborate rites of passage, obelisks, arches, columns, fountains and a beautiful palace in the heart of the leading city.

The deep attachment of market liberalism to this old imagery of sovereignty is obvious. It clings to the language of the free market and the tough state, negative liberty *and* political discipline, and in this respect it is a self-contradictory project. Like lovers who thrive on interminable squabbles, the market and the state both require the other, but neither can live peacefully with the other. The key point is that market liberalism is incapable of actualizing the 'libertarian' values it affirms. It is hoist with its own petard of 'freedom of choice', and that is why its critics must open their eyes wider. They need to give their criticisms of market liberalism more bite and public appeal by emphasizing not only that markets fail to guarantee the open expression and representation of opinions, but also that market liberalism is in love with arcane and 'invisible' state power, which also contradicts freedom of communication among a plurality of citizens.

Public Service Media?

The idea of public service must be detached from the idea of public monopoly, yet remain public service in the true sense. The only way of achieving this is to create new kinds of institution.

Raymond Williams, 1962

Two profound weaknesses on the side of the critics of 'deregulation' have so far been emphasized in this essay: their neglect of the self-contradictory and self-paralysing tendencies of market-based communications media, and the insufficient attention they pay to the growth of state censorship. The case against market liberalism in favour of public service communications is weakened further by a third, related blindspot: its unconvincing attempt to justify publicly the public service model against its enemies.

It is obvious that if communications media are defensible as a public service then their role and significance must be clearly and plausibly stated. Unfortunately, the contemporary case for public service media is trapped in a profound legitimation problem. Like trade unions, political parties and legislatures, public service media have become deeply uncertain about the scope and nature of their contemporary role in representing their constituents in the state and civil society. Public service media are caught up in a broader malaise, in which older forms of representation are weakened and Balkanized.[106]

Symptomatic of this malaise is the manner in which

---

[106] See Pierre Rosanvallon, 'Malaise dans la représentation', in François Furet et al., *La République du Centre* (Paris, 1988).

public service devotees rest their case upon a self-paralysing tautology: public service media are viewed as a synonym for institutions like RAI, the BBC, and the Länder broadcasters in Germany, whose reputation, size, diversity and privileged position enable them to attract talent, to innovate and to produce balanced, quality programming. Public service is 'the broad commitment to provide and to protect mixed and complementary programming schedules. It includes a commitment to certain minority programes and to covering, as far as possible, different genres of programme making. Within each genre – whether within drama, current affairs, comedy, children's programmes or continuing education – there is a full range of programming, a demonstrably broad church. Public service broadcasting is driven by higher aspirations than solely to provide entertainment. Public service broadcasting is the attempt to make quality popular programmes. It does justice to human experience. It deals in more than stereotypes. It adds to the quality of people's lives. Its programme genres reflect the complexity of human beings.'[107]

The important practical achievements of quality broadcasting in this sense should not be underestimated.[108] The twentieth-century attempt to provide a service of mixed programmes on national

---

[107] Interview with Jonathan Powell, Programme Controller, BBC1, London (2 November 1989).

[108] The most sophisticated defences of the public service broadcasting model are: Paddy Scannell, 'Public Service Broadcasting: History of a Concept', in A. Goodwin and G. Whannel (eds), *Understanding Television* (London, 1989); Paddy Scannell, 'Public Service Broadcasting and Modern Public Life', *Media, Culture and Society*, 11 (1989), pp. 135–66; and Paddy Scannell and David Cardiff, *A Social History of British Broadcasting*, vol. 1 (Oxford, 1990).

radio and television channels available to all, often in the face of technical problems and pressing commercial considerations, has arguably widened the horizons of public awareness of social life. For a time, the 'provision of basic services [*Grundversorgung*]' (as the German Federal Constitutional Court puts it) helped to *decommodify* the media. It diminished the role of accounting, corporate *chutzpah* and general greed as the principal qualities necessary to media management. It has enforced specific national rules covering such matters as the amount and type of advertising, political access, balanced news coverage, and quotas of foreign programming. It succeeded for a time in protecting employment levels in the national broadcasting industries of countries such as Canada, Australia, Britain and the Federal Republic of Germany. The public service model has legitimized the presence of ordinary citizens in programmes dealing with controversial issues and problems; it has helped to make idiomatic, conversational styles respectable; and, significantly, it has publicized the pleasures of ordinariness, creating entertainment out of citizens playing games, talking about their experiences or taking delight in events as disparate as football and tennis matches, religious ceremonies and dancing to the current top ten.

There are nevertheless problems with the argument that existing public service media are a bulwark of freedom against the confusions and limitations of commercial media. To treat existing public service media reactively, as the paragon of 'quality', 'balance' and 'universal accessibility', is myopic. It bears a striking parallel to the first defensive responses to the early market liberal attacks on the welfare state. The early campaigns, using slogans such as 'Save the Welfare State!' and 'Stop the Cuts!', implied support for institutions unworthy of full support and, for that reason among others, they have failed to outmanoeuvre the market liberals' subsequent restructuring and (partial) dismantling of the welfare state.[109] By analogy, conservative defences of public service media – lifting eyes towards the statue of Lord Reith – are inadequate, and are likely to fail for reasons to do with the internal weaknesses of the public service model.

The prevailing definition of this model underestimates the ways in which technological change – the advent of cable, satellite, television, community radio – has slowly but surely destroyed the traditional argument that the scarcity of available spectrum frequencies blesses public service broadcasting with the status of a 'natural monopoly' within the boundaries of a given nation-state. This argument is no longer true. The reigning definition of public service media also makes the strategic mistake of justifying itself publicly in the rhetoric of 'quality'. Public service advocates frequently talk about 'preserving quality programmes' – which normally are defined loosely (according to a media friend of mine) as polished, stylish and challenging productions. Alas, loose talk of quality is vulnerable to the retort that the concept of quality is riddled with semantic ambiguity.[110] The late eighteenth-century dis-

---

[109] Pierre Rosanvallon, 'The Decline of Social Visibility', in Keane, *Civil Society and the State. New European Perspectives*, pp. 199–220; and my *Democracy and Civil Society*.

[110] The best recent discussion of the semantic ambiguity of the term quality is Geoff Mulgan, 'Television's Holy Grail: Seven Types of Quality', in Geoff Mulgan (ed.), *The Question of Quality* (London, 1990), pp. 4–32. On the slow 'democratization' of the eighteenth-century meaning of quality as an attribute of civilized life, see Kenneth Cmiel, *Democratic Eloquence. The Fight over Popular Speech in Nineteenth-Century America* (New York, 1990).

tinction between 'persons and things of quality' and 'the vulgar' has broken down. What constitutes 'good' or 'quality' media is now deeply controversial, even though everybody is generally in favour of it. The word 'quality' has no objective basis, only a plurality of ultimately clashing, contradictory meanings amenable to public manipulation.

Some defenders of the public service model, for example, view quality in terms of the ability of the media to bind together disparate and fragmented audiences into a classless community of individuals who feel others to be their equals, with whom they can share news of events, television characters and fictional narratives, and of whom they can freely ask such questions as 'Did you read this?' or 'Did you see that?'[111] From a quite different angle, the quality of public service media is sometimes justified in terms of its ability to best express certain producer–defined technical qualities, such as superior camerawork and lighting, intelligently written scripts, professional direction, superb acting, effective narratives and clear and comprehensible ideas. Other commentators consider media products to be of high quality insofar as they stand the test of time; high quality books or films or television programmes – *Bonanza* and the *Bill Cosby Show*, for example – are those which outlive their moment of birth, escape the limits of their context and establish a strong reputation among subsequent audiences or even generations. By contrast, post-modernists and others think of quality in diametrically opposed terms: television in particular is praised for being at the cutting edge of the deliberately superficial 'three minute culture' and its dizzying swirl of disjointed and entertaining images. Post-modernism

---

[111] See James Carey, *Communication as Culture: Essays on Media and Society* (London, 1989).

celebrates the relacement of narrative with flow, sequence with randomness, connection with disconnection. It welcomes the arrival of quick-cut pop videos, short sound bites, split-second photo opportunities and situation comedies – the most popular television form – which so rapidly serve up so many 'situations' that audiences cannot remember what they are laughing at.

Pro-marketeers propose yet another view of quality. Seizing upon – and reinforcing – the semantic ambiguity of the term, they criticize the public service model as confused and patronizing. They attack public service devotees as snobs who arrogantly assume their freedom of expression to be the guarantee of quality, and who thereby deny publics what they often like best: a wide choice of fruit that is ripe and juicy. Market liberals assume that audiences are sovereign consumers, and that the only workable index of quality is their pattern of choices, that is, the degree of popularity of newspapers, radio and television programmes; effective demand, the willingness of individuals to purchase a product, is the criterion of its quality. The pro-market rhetoric about quality contains a definite libertarian ring. Murdoch claims, for instance, that 'quality is in the eye of the beholder, or in the current debate . . . , the propagandist.' This leads him to a cunningly unconventional – market-orientated – definition of the public service model: 'anybody who, within the law of the land, provides a service which the public wants at a price it can afford is providing a public service.'[112]

---

[112] Ibid., p. 4; cf. the virtually identical remarks of Roberto Giovalli, Head of Programme Planning for Fininvest: 'My concern is to give people what they want, not what improves them. Television does not make the times. It follows them. Or at least it mirrors them' (cited in the *Guardian* (20 March 1989), p. 25).

Those who ignore the public appeal of this kind of rhetoric are naive. They overlook the ways in which the alleged 'balance', 'quality' standards and universalism of existing public service media are routinely perceived by certain audiences as 'unrepresentative'. The totality of output of mixed programmes in nationally networked channels cannot add up to a complete world. Their repertoire cannot exhaust the multitude of opinions in a complex (if less than fully pluralist) society in motion. The public service claim to representativeness is a defence of *virtual* representation of a fictive whole, a resort to programming which *simulates* the actual opinions and tastes of *some* of those to whom it is directed. That is why the public service claim to 'inform all of the people all of the time' triggers a constant stream of complaints: public service media normally fail to satisfy enthusiasts of particular types of programmes.

Music is a pertinent example. Although, for obvious reasons, music has always occupied the bulk of radio time, it has proved impossible in the long term to provide programming with general appeal on public service radio because a common musical culture has never existed. Different music appeals to different publics, whose dislikes are often as strong as their likes, and that is why the twentieth-century history of radio has resulted in a gradual fragmentation of mass audiences into different taste publics.[113] Public service media corset audiences and violate their own principle of

---

[113] Paddy Scannell, 'Music for the Multitude? The Dilemmas of the BBC's Music Policy, 1923–1946', *Media, Culture and Society*, 3 (1982), pp. 243–60. The decline of the paternalist tradition in British radio is also well examined in Richard Barbrook, 'Melodies or Rhythms?: The Competition for the Greater London FM Radio Licence', *Popular Music*, vol. 9, no. 2 (1990), pp. 203–19.

equality of access for all to entertainment, current affairs and cultural resources in a common public domain. For reasons of a commitment to 'balance', government pressures and threatened litigation, the public service representation of such topics as sexuality, politics and violence also tends to be timid. Certain things cannot be transmitted, or not in a particular way. When they are transmitted, their disturbing, troublesome or outrageous implications are often closed off. And public service media – here they are no different from their commercial competitors – distribute entitlements to speak and to be heard and seen unevenly. They too develop a cast of regulars – reporters, presenters, commentators, academic experts, businesspeople, politicians, trade unionists, cultural authorities – who appear as accredited representatives of public experience and taste by virtue of their regular appearance on the media.

All this is grist for the mill of the marketeers, and that is why defenders of the public sevice model who talk only about preserving the 'quality' and 'balance' of the existing system make a crucial strategic mistake. They allow the market liberals to elope with the old vocabulary of 'liberty of the press'. 'Save the public service model' is a self-defeating position in the fight against market liberalism. It concedes too much. The rich, if histrionic vocabulary of market liberalism (freedom from state control, freedom of individual choice, quality through diversity) should be neither haughtily neglected nor accepted uncritically. The pseudo-libertarian appeals of market liberalism are central to its overall goal of controlling the present and the future – of commercializing the media of communication and subjecting them to new forms of state control – by redefining and monopolizing the dominant, collectively shared sense of the historical past. Market liberals are attempting to rewrite history. They aim to brand public regulation as paternalistic, as timocratic, as an assault on the old American and European heritage of liberty from state control. This fight to rewrite history from above serves as an important reminder that traditions do not grow on trees, but are made, unmade and remade constantly. It reminds us that those who control the production of traditions, who dominate the present and manipulate the past, are likely also to control the future. And it reminds us that the debate over who shall inherit the old European and American vocabulary of 'liberty of the press' is long overdue, and that gaining the upper hand in these controversies is imperative for the survival and development of a public service communications system which resolves the flaws of market liberalism, and which, consequently, is more genuinely open and pluralistic, and therefore accessible to citizens of all persuasions.

But what would a redefined, broadened and more accessible and accountable public service model look like in practice? What would be its guiding principles? How could a revised public service model deal with the self-paralysing tendencies of market-based communications and the new forms of politicial censorship in democratic regimes? How could a revised public service model legitimate itself more convincingly than at present? In short, what could 'liberty of the press' come to mean at the end of the twentieth century?

It is obvious that a renewed public service system of communications would need to be clear from the outset about its guiding principles and strategies. It should attempt to counter head-on the market liberal strategy of the free market guided by the tough state. For the reasons explained earlier in this essay, public service communications should not be treated as a synonym for market competition. Murdoch's view that 'anybody who, within the law of the land, provides a service which the public wants at a price it can afford is providing a public service' must be rejected, since it cannot deal with the problem of market censorship. For that reason as well, public service communications should not be treated (as they are in the United States, for example) as a poor mimicry of the market – as a second-rate attempt to replicate artificially the production methods and programming schedules that would be provided by a genuine market in communications, were it given half a chance. The American system of non-commercial broadcasting combines instructional radio and television, which originated in the 1950s, with the Public Broadcasting Service (PBS) established by the Public Broadcasting Act of 1967. Denied adequate funding since its inception, the public service model has suffered a permanent identity crisis. How can its funding base be rendered secure? Given that it is partly supported by tax dollars, should it seek to adopt an expansive programming strategy aimed at the broadest possible audiences? Should it avoid controversial programmes so as to escape 'punishment' by an incumbent administration? How 'commercial' should the system be? How should it be managed? How representative are the boards of local public broadcasting stations? And, fundamentally, should public broadcasting exist at all?

Public service media cannot rise above these primitive budgetary and administrative questions if they are viewed as mere ancillaries of market competition. Public service media also cannot operate effectively if they are treated (like public parks or ancient monuments) as a 'merit good', that is, as providers of worthy programmes for minorities which involve 'knowledge, culture, criticism and experiment' (Lord Quinton), and which can find no outlet in the mainstream. Public service media should certainly serve minorities and circulate knowledge and culture, and stimulate criticism and experimentation, even slapping the face of public taste as often as possible. But they must do more than that. Public service media should build on the decommodifying achievements of the original public service model, all the while acknowledging that it has now slipped into a profound and irreversible crisis. A fundamentally revised public service model should aim to facilitate a genuine commonwealth of forms of life, tastes and opinions, to empower a plurality of citizens who are governed neither by despotic states nor by market forces. It should circulate to them a wide variety of opinions. It should enable them to live democratically within the framework of multilayered constitutional states which are held accountable to their citizens, who work and consume, live and love, quarrel and compromise within independent, self-organizing civil societies which underpin and transcend the narrow boundaries of state institutions.[114] The public service principle proposed here has old roots traceable to the English and American Revolutions. A glimmer of it was expressed in the events surrounding Erskine's

---

[114] Compare the sketches provided in Graham Murdock and Peter Golding, 'Information Poverty and Political Inequality: Citizenship in the Age of Privatized Communications', *Journal of Communication*, vol. 39, no. 3 (Summer 1989), pp. 180–95; and Jeffrey B. Abramson et al., *The Electronic Commonwealth. The Impact of New Media Technologies on Democratic Politics* (New York, 1988).

defence of Tom Paine: communications media should be for the public use and enjoyment of all citizens and not for the private gain or profit of political rulers or businesses.

Government in the sunshine

A state is bound to be more dangerous if it is not governed openly by the people, but secretly by political forces that are not widely known or understood

Andrei Sakharov, 1987

But the question remains: what would a public service communications system look like in practice? How would it be funded? Through which political and legal strategies could it be developed?

One priority is the exposure and repeal of the censorial methods of contemporary state power. In view of the growth of lawless and invisible government, the onus must be placed on governments everywhere to justify publicly *any* interference with *any* part of the circulation of opinions. Government must not be considered the legitimate trustee of information. Erskine, in Tom Paine's defence, said it all: 'Other liberties are held *under* government, but the liberty of opinion keeps governments themselves in due subjection to their duties.'

This principle, when brought to bear upon the forms of political censorship outlined above, points to the need for a new constitutional settlement in all Western democracies (and in the regimes of central and eastern Europe, presently preoccupied with the difficult business of constitution-making and dismantling totalitarian structures). Freedom and equality of communication requires legal protection and, where necessary, a written constitution. A great variety of legal means can help to promote freedom of expression and access to information among transacting citizens. Where a country has a written constitution, freedom of expression and of the media should be protected within it as well as within other national legislation. The principle that freedom is the rule and limitation the exception should be adhered to.

The American First Amendment ('Congress shall make no law . . . abridging the freedom of speech or of the press') still serves as the prototype of such legislation. It certainly contains several troubling conceptual flaws, which have become the subject of intense controversy.[115] Two centuries of constitutional adjudication have clouded an Amendment whose wording appeared to be shiningly clear. As Alexander Hamilton and others predicted, it has become buried under piles of antecedent case law which confronts each new justice with the awkward task of tip-toeing through fine distinctions and picayune details, and of accounting for prior decisions, rather than interpreting and applying the Amendment directly. Many examples leap to mind. One continuing source of debate has been whether 'freedom of the press' and 'freedom of speech', both of which are protected by the Amendment, imply separate systems of differing constitutional protection or are simply reiterations of one indivisible freedom. Another

---

[115] See William W. van Alstyne, *Interpretations of the First Amendment* (Durham, NC, 1984); and Ronald K. L. Collins and David M. Skover (eds), 'The First Amendment in an Age of Paratroopers', *Texas Law Review*, 68 (May 1990), pp. 1087–193.

dispute revolves around the issue of whether and to what extent the Amendment covers not only the press deriving from Gutenberg, but also radio, television, computers and other twentieth-century electronic communications.

There have been additional disputes about federalism, including whether the latitudes of federal and state rulings on the scope of freedom of expression are identical and, if not, whether and to what extent the former should prevail. The *kind* of speech referred to within the Amendment – obscene or religious, commercial or political, private or public – has been hotly debated. On this question, a literal interpretation of the Amendment has never commanded a majority of the Supreme Court. The relatively straightforward case of a person knowingly shouting 'Fire!' in a crowded theatre, for the perverse pleasure of causing a panic and watching others being trampled in a frenzied crowd, has been interpreted through the formula proposed by Justice Holmes: 'The question in every case is whether the words used are used in such circumstances and are of such a nature as to create a clear and present danger that they will bring about the substantive evils that Congress has a right to prevent.'[116] The formula subsequently proposed by Judge Learned Hand represents a sharpening of the same principle: 'In each case [courts] must ask whether the gravity of the "evil", discounted by its improbability, justifies such invasion of free speech as is necessary to avoid the danger.'[117] Notwithstanding such efforts to define prohibited speech, Mapplethorpe photographs of male nudes, burning Old Glory and

---

[116] *Schenk* v. *United States*, 249 US 47, 52 (1919).
[117] *Dennis* v. *United States*, 341 US 494, 510 (1951).

draft registration cards, and 'inciting or producing imminent lawless action' by marching through Jewish neighbourhoods shouting Nazi slogans continue to provoke red-hot controversies.

The adoption of a *corporate* view of press freedom, applying the press clause of the First Amendment to justify special privileges for the 'institution' of the media, has been resisted on the grounds that freedom of the press arose historically as an *individual* liberty, and that freedom of speech and of the press remain 'fundamental personal rights' (Chief Justice Hughes). Further arguments have been sparked by the problem of compulsory disclosures, for example, whether journalists can be threatened with fines or prison terms and made to disclose information which was entrusted to them in confidence in their professional capacity as journalists. And there has been continuing controversy about whether the First Amendment was intended as a *defence* against government, that is, as a shield to defend citizens and the media against prior restraints on their power of expression, or whether the clause can also be invoked as a weapon for ensuring 'freedom of information', that is, as a means of *attacking* state censorship.

The pathbreaking case of *Richmond, Inc* v. *Virginia* (448 US 555 [1980]) settled this last controversy in favour of the view that the principle of freedom of communication can be used as a sword against state power. It pointed to the vital need, in any democracy, for legislation enforcing a citizens' right of reply in the media against their governments. Suing governments for damages is prohibitively expensive for the majority of citizens. Legal backing is required which allows anyone injured by offensive or inaccurate statements the right of reply in the same communications outlet in which such statements have been made.[118] There are traps here, admittedly. In France, for example, state officials have a right to insist that published information concerning them be rectified. This has led to an abuse of the right of reply by imposing on the media an obligation to publish extensive government reports and even propaganda in response to alleged misrepresentation. Individual citizens nevertheless have a right of reply against government. Any citizen can insist on being given space to answer coverage which refers to her or him. Publishers' failure to print the reply within three days is subject to penalties of fines and imprisonment. The right of reply of citizens is considered absolute: it is not necessary that a citizen should have been defamed or that the statement actually be untrue.

Freedom of expression among citizens supposes not only the power to impart points of view against government. In addition it requires the power to *seek* points of view. This 'right to know' requires solid institutional support. Of special importance would be the abolition of 'lobby systems', various forms of which presently function to limit publicity surrounding potentially controversial events in favour of selected journalists and current government policies. The (further) development of independently minded and publicly accessible standing committees – of the legislative, investigatory or advisory kind anticipated in the Bundestag and the American Congress – could ensure more effective scrutiny and control of both the executive and the invisible branches of the democratic Leviathan.

---

[118] See Jerome A. Barron, *Public Rights and the Private Press* (Toronto, 1981) and *Freedom of the Press for Whom? The Right of Access to Mass Media* (New York, 1973).

The 'right to know' also requires firm legal recognition and protection, since it is fundamental to ensuring open and publicly accountable government. Among the pathbreaking efforts to do this is the hard look doctrine, first articulated in the United States in the case of *Greater Boston Television Co.* v. *FCC* (1970), and later moulded into the 1977 Government in the Sunshine Act.[119] The doctrine grew out of widespread complaints that parts of the state were not compelled to speak openly to the relationship between their own and wider interests. Hard look doctrine is suspicious of closed bargaining and *ex parte* negotiations. It aims to make state institutions accountable to their citizens without producing administrative overload. The doctrine seeks a path between so-called 'substantial evidence' rules, which require policymakers to explain and justify their every move, and more lenient 'kid glove' standards, which oblige decision makers to explain only the logic underpinning the decisions they reach. Hard look doctrine circumscribes what can be dealt with collectively when citizens cannot be present at hearings, and provides that all other meetings of an agency be open to public observation unless the matter is statutorily exempted. It specifies the procedures for closing meetings, and requires that records of such meetings be kept. The doctrine lays down procedures for guaranteeing public access to these records, and specifies the ground rules

---

[119] *Greater Boston Television Co.* v. *FCC*, 444 F. 2d. 841 (DC Cir. 1970) 403 US 923 (1971), p. 851; D. Welborn et al., *Implementation and Effects of the Government in the Sunshine Act*, Draft Report for the Administrative Conference of the United States (Washington, DC, 1984); and Ian Harden and Norman Lewis, *The Noble Lie. The British Constitution and the Rule of Law* (London, 1986), especially chapters 8–10.

for judicial review of alleged violations of the doctrine itself.

The various Freedom of Information Acts already in existence (for example, those in the United States, Canada and Australia) are guided by similar aims. They seek to empower citizens against their political representatives by facilitating citizens' access to information held in the files of state (and civil) authorities and, thus, by increasing the quantity and quality of the flow of information between government and citizens, and among citizens themselves. In practice, things are often different because the scope of the legislation is too narrow. The Access to Information Act in Canada is a case in point. Many categories of information are unavailable for public scrutiny: information obtained originally from a foreign government or another provincial government; the bulk of sensitive commercial data; records of the operation of the federal Cabinet; and information that is capable of harming trade, defence or diplomatic interests or pertains to the enforcement of the law. There are difficulties, too, surrounding the implementation of freedom of information legislation, which requires the development of a public record-keeping system that can balance the competing requirements of effective administration (minimizing what the Canadians call 'paperburden'), public access and the safe-keeping of archival records.[120]

Legislation covering data protection is also an impor-

---

[120] See James Cornford, 'Official Secrecy and Freedom of Information', in Richard Holme and Michael Elliott (eds), *1688–1988. Time for a New Constitution* (Basingstoke and London, 1988), pp. 143–66; and the fine study by Patrick Birkinshaw, *Freedom of Information. The Law, the Practice and the Ideal* (London, 1988).

tant means of preventing political censorship. The principle of data protection was first enshrined in West German and Scandinavian legislation in the early 1970s. It developed out of concerns over the growing power of computer systems to manipulate information without individuals and groups knowing what data is filed and the purposes for which it is used. The European Convention on Data Protection, which came into force in October 1985, provides an international legal framework for individual countries to adopt. Most national data protection legislation deals only with information stored in computers – in some countries the law extends to records kept manually – and it often excludes rights of access to the records of government departments dealing with such matters as social security, taxation, police and immigration. The point underpinning data protection legislation is nevertheless serious and important, if paradoxical: individual citizens require guaranteed access to their personal files held by state (and civil) 'data users' in order to ensure the *privacy* of that information. Such legislation aims to prevent unauthorized access to personal information as well as to enable individuals to certify that their personal data is accurate, up to date and actually relevant for the purpose for which it is filed. These points are well summarized in Article 1 of the French Law on Informatics and Liberty (1978): 'Computer science must be at the service of each citizen; its development has to operate within the framework of international co-operation; it should not damage human identity, human rights, private life or individual and public liberties.'

Rethinking Sovereignty

There can be no human society without government, no government without sovereignty, no sovereignty without infallibility.

Joseph de Maistre, 1821

There remains the vexed question of how to deal with the unaccountability of supra-national political institutions. Their expanding power could be rendered more accountable by subjecting them to various forms of parliamentary supervision. These could include strengthened standing committees, closer cooperation among national legislatures and, in turn, their coordination with supra-national legislatures – such as the European Parliament – whose strengthening, contrary to some expressed doubts, might well contribute to the reviviscence of their national counterparts.

Another potentially fruitful option is suggested by proposals for developing an international civil society.[121] The fullest possible implementation of high

[121] Compare the constitutionalist (neo-Kantian) interpretation of Ralf Dahrendorf, 'Citizenship and the Modern Social Conflict', in Holme and Elliott, *1688–1988. Time for a New Constitution*, pp. 112–25, and my interview, 'Decade of the Citizen', the *Guardian* (1 August 1990); my *Democracy and Civil Society*; and Morten Ougaard, 'The Internationalisation of Civil Society', Center for Udviklingsforskning (Copenhagen, June 1990). There are also stimulating remarks on the possibility of an international public sphere in Nicholas Garnham, 'The Media and the Public Sphere. Part 2', paper presented to the conference 'Habermas and the Public Sphere', the University of North Carolina at Chapel Hill (8–10 September 1989); and

international standards governing citizens' rights of communication is clearly important. Article 19 of the Universal Declaration of Human Rights is an example: 'Everyone has the right to freedom of opinion and expression; this right includes the freedom to hold opinions without interference and to seek, receive and impart information and ideas through any media and regardless of frontiers.'

Declarations of this kind are fuelled by the ideal of a new global information and communication order – a concept mentioned for the first time in a UN General Assembly resolution in 1978 and formulated in documents such as the MacBride Commission's *Many Voices, One World* (1980). It also tends to be supported by the development, since the 1960s, of electronic and satellite technologies, which feed upon the economies of scale inherent in broadcasting, where the marginal cost of an extra viewer is zero. Satellite communications enable users to fly over and around the walls of the nation-state. These technologies are able to transfer voices, data, texts and images swiftly over long distances and to large geographic areas. The relayed information can take the form of television or radio broadcasts, telefax messages and telephone conversations, or it can be specific data, related to financial markets, professional conferences, sporting events or weather information, often collected by computer databases at both ends of the link.

Such developments in global communications media,

Daniel C. Hallin and Paulo Mancini, 'Summits and the Constitution of an International Public Sphere: The Reagan–Gorbachev Meetings as Televised Media Events', unpublished paper, University of California, San Diego and Università degli Studi di Perugia (September 1990).

in theory at least, make the world smaller and more open. These media operate to an extent as a global Fourth Estate – as during the recent 'velvet revolutions' in central-eastern Europe.[122] Telephones, fax machines, photocopiers, electronic bulletin boards and video and audio recordings, especially when linked to global telecommunications networks, are now used world-wide to subvert repressive governments. Some states are being forced to relinquish some of their powers, as the growth of an unusual crop of political leaders practising the art of dismantling despotic regimes indicates.[123] Developments in global communications theoretically ensure that events anywhere can be reported anywhere else on radio within minutes; on television within hours. But theory and practice are often far apart. Government regulation, combined with the high costs of installing telecommunications equipment and providing publicly accessible terminals, prevents citizens of most countries from accessing such global telecommunications networks as teleconferencing and electronic mail systems. Meanwhile, private broadcast news has become a global business, like the music industry, with its own 'Top 10' and an inevitable streamlining of opinions and tastes. A few major organizations control the newsflow. Syndicators such as Visnews and WTN guarantee that wider and wider audiences get to read, see or hear the same stories.[124]

---

[122] Timothy Garton Ash, 'The Revolution of the Magic Lantern', *New York Review of Books*, 18 January 1990, pp. 44–5.

[123] John Keane, 'The Politics of Retreat', *The Political Quarterly*, vol. 61, no. 3 (July–September 1990), pp. 340–52.

[124] Stanley Baran and Roger Wallis, *The Known World of Broadcast News. International News and the Electronic Media* (London, 1990).

Other problems concerning the ownership and operation of global communications media are emerging. A few wealthy countries monopolize the ownership, launching and control of satellites, due to the high costs incurred in purchasing and maintaining the technology. There is an absence of common technical standards which would ensure the easy exchange of information between different satellite communication channels. Problems also arise from the limited number of satellites that can be launched into a geostationary orbit, from which they operate as transmitters for certain geographic areas; at present, satellite orbit slots and frequencies are the subject of intense international dispute between those who consider that space belongs to the earth in common and those governments which assume that their more powerful number should decide. And there are emerging controversies about whether satellites should be used for secret intelligence gathering, military photography and telephone tapping.

For these reasons, the development of an international civil society cannot be left to legislators or technologies alone. It also requires militant efforts to enrich *from below* the flows of information among communicating citizens, regardless of the nation-states within which they live. To some degree, this requirement can be satisfied by intelligent, public-spirited forms of journalism, which have emerged in recent years as a separate and specialized branch of the media. So-called quality investigative journalism came to the fore during the Watergate scandal, but it has long been a feature of the type of cosmopolitan journalism exemplified by *Der Spiegel* and the *New Statesman and Society*. Quality journalism rejects tabloid newspaper tactics, whose golden rules are: please the news desk; get front page coverage and stay in front of everyone else; reflect the prejudices of readers; defend nationalist hype and page three pin-ups; fight for 'the scandal of gay vicar' and other sensational exclusives with as little legal comeback as possible; remain emotionally uninvolved in any and every story; if necessary, invade privacy on a scale that would impress a burglar, all the while explaining to the interviewees that their willingness to cooperate will help others in a similar plight. High quality investigative journalism lives by different rules.[125] It seeks to counteract the secretive and noisy arrogance of the democratic Leviathan. It involves the patient investigation and exposure of political corruption, misconduct and mismanagement. It clings to the old maxim of American muckrakers – 'the news is what someone, somewhere, *doesn't* want to see printed.' It aims to sting political power, to tame its arrogance by extending the limits of public controversy and widening citizens' informed involvement in the public spheres of civil society.

An international civil society of freely communicating citizens can develop if public encouragement and material support are also given to a wide variety of non-governmental associations working to combat political censorship. In recent years, such organizations have become a feature of the 'globalization' of power. Most of them are little known and struggle for survival under harsh financial and political pressures. Such organizations are of two types: those nationally based, such

---

[125] A fine example is Neal Ascherson, *Games with Shadows* (London, 1988); see also Duncan Campbell, 'Paradoxes of Secrecy', *Index on Censorship*, vol. 17, no. 8 (September 1988), pp. 16–19; and my sketch of the twentieth-century decline of 'fellow-travelling political journalism' in 'Sovjetska svoboda?', *Vestnik*, vol 8, no. 2 (1987), pp. 7–8.

as Index on Censorship, Wolnosc i Pokój and the Alliance for Justice, which strive to monitor and to document the performance of governments and to mobilize public opinion in support of their findings; and those with affiliated bodies or memberships in several countries, such as International PEN, Greenpeace, Amnesty International, Ecoropa, the Helsinki Citizens' Assembly, the International Federation of Actors and the International Commission of Jurists.

Ultimately, this bundle of proposals can be plausible only if the thorny old *problématique* of the sovereignty of the state is confronted head on, and displaced. Defenders of political censorship react sharply to such proposals. They are adamant that the state must always be empowered to eliminate the 'Worms within the Entrails' of the body politic (Hobbes). Under emergency conditions, citizens must confront the state in awe and fear. The presumption in resistance must always be against them: 'When the final and absolute authority of the state executive is threatened, and when push comes to shove', a defender of nation-state sovereignty might insist, 'freedom of communication is a dispensable luxury. Erskine was wrong. Freedom of expression can produce disorder and even civil war. All liberties, including the "liberty of the press", must therefore be held *under* government. Blackstone was right: the liberty of the media consists in "laying no *previous* restraints upon publications, and not in freedom from seizure for criminal matter when published".'

Here the argument traps itself within the chain of reasoning of Joseph de Maistre's *Du Pape* (1821): 'There can be no human society without government, no government without sovereignty, no sovereignty without infallibility.' Those who still assert such views need to be answered in the toughest terms. The defence of state censorship by market liberals and others is a nonsense, because it rests upon the obsolete principle of executive sovereignty. The 'sovereign state' is today under siege from two sides. At home it is subject to important centrifugal tendencies, bearing especially on the shifting boundaries between the state and civil society, itself subject to centrifugal and internationalizing trends.[126] In foreign affairs, states are ever more intermeshed in transnational frameworks of macrodecision making.[127] Ever more executive decisions are limited or foreclosed by the membership of states in military arrangements and intergovernmental organizations such as the IMF, the UN and the EEC, as well as by the investment decisions of transnational corporations. Both trends are in a real sense synthesized by the invention and deployment of nuclear weapons. Their capacity to annihilate both attacker and defender under battle conditions arguably puts an end to the independence abroad and exclusive jurisdiction at home of all nation-states.

---

[126] See David Beetham, 'The Future of the Nation State', in Gregor McLennan, David Held and Stuart Hall (eds), *The Idea of the Modern State* (Milton Keynes, 1984); my *Democracy and Civil Society*; and the introductory remarks to John Keane (ed.), *Civil Society and the State. New European Perspectives*.

[127] See K. Kaiser, 'Transnational Relations as a Threat to the Democratic Process', in R. O. Keohane and J. S. Nye (eds), *Transnational Relations and World Politics* (Cambridge, Mass., 1972); David Held, 'Sovereignty, National Politics and the Global System', in *Political Theory and the Modern State* (Cambridge, 1989), pp. 214–42; and Margaret Blunden, 'Collaboration and Competition in European Weapons Procurement: The Issue of Democratic Accountability', *Defense Analysis*, vol. 5, no. 4 (1990), pp. 291–304.

'But' – interrupts the critic – 'these forces working against unlimited and indivisible executive state power should not be exaggerated. The end of the modern nation-state is not nigh. The so-called "globalization" process is highly uneven.' There is real force in this objection. The extent to which the 'sovereignty' of a particular nation-state is presently eroding depends not only on its past history (for example, whether and to what extent it ever enjoyed 'sovereign status'). It also depends on such contemporary factors as its position in the force-fields of global power politics, its place in the world economy, its implication in international agencies and legal systems, and the strength and effervescence of the domestic and international civil societies on which its power structures are based. And there are circumstances, as in the newly emerging republics in the Soviet Union, where the regaining of national sovereignty, paradoxically, is a basic condition of citizens participating more equally and effectively in the current supranational trends.

Nevertheless – the critic needs to be told – the argument that sovereignty does not and cannot reside in the hands of state executives must now be taken seriously. The modern idea of the centralized, sovereign nation-state, a 'national community of sentiments secured by military strength and economic interests (Weber) which is both independent of any external authority and capable of governing the territory and population it monopolizes, is in deep trouble. The governmental bodies of nation-state communities no longer (if they ever fully did) exclusively determine the lives of their citizens. Our globe is beginning to resemble the *form* of the medieval world, in which the political powers of the monarch or prince were forced to share authority with a variety of subordinate and higher powers. 'Sovereignty' is becoming a decadent fiction – if still a most useful fiction in the hands of undemocratic forces, who insist that there are times when the state be granted the plenitude of power, and who cry, with Dante, that the *maxime unum* is the *maxime bonum*.

The 'decline of sovereignty' has profound implications for a revised theory of freedom of communication. It forces a fundamental rethinking of the classical theory of 'liberty of the press', which viewed communications systems only within the framework of the system of single nation-states. It highlights the distance between the early modern period and today's world. It forces consideration of the rise of globally organized media companies, whose operations routinely break the strait-jacket of the nation-state and its domestic markets. And it reminds us of the importance of the growing impact of supra–national legal and political arrangements, and of the slow and delicate growth of an international civil society.

The decline of sovereignty also has profound implications for radical strategies of enhancing 'liberty of the press' at the end of the twentieth century. The traditional twentieth-century view of radical opposition – the revolutionary strategy of seizing state power, if need be through the use of violence – was cast in terms of 'capturing' the General Post Office, 'seizing' radio and television stations and other 'centres' of state power and influence. The aim was to prevent counter-revolution and to plant the seeds of the future society. This thought informed the Soviet Government decree of mid-November 1917, curtailing freedom of the press. 'The state is only a transitional institution which we are obliged to use in the revolutionary struggle in order to crush our opponents forcibly.' Couching its argument in these terms, the fledgling Bolshevik Government proceeded to silence its 'bourgeois' opponents (many of whom were in fact socialists and social democrats) with the following explanation: 'The suppression of the bourgeois papers was caused not only by purely fighting requirements in the period of counter-revolutionary attempts, but likewise as a necessary temporary measure for the establishment of a new regime in the sphere of the press, under which the capitalist proprietors of printing plants and newsprint would not be able to become autocratic beguilers of public opinion . . . The re-establishment of the so-called freedom of the Press; viz. the simple return of printing offices and paper to capitalists, poisoners of the people's conscience, would be an unpardonable surrender to the will of capital, that is to say, a counter-revolutionary measure.'[128]

The decline of state sovereignty renders *implausible* this strategy of 'capturing' the 'centres' of power and communication which – as the labyrinthine structures of political censorship discussed above indicate – are in fact tending to become more dispersed. The highly differentiated character of democratic regimes provides the reminder that there is simply no single centre of state power which could be 'occupied' and used to transform radically civil society with the help of the means of communication. Not only that, but insofar as 'the state' is insufficiently in one place to be 'seized', the strategy of monopolizing the means of communication for radical purposes is rendered *unnecessary*. The often uncoor-

---

[128] 'The Central Executive Committee Discusses the Decree on the Press', *Delo Naroda*, 200 (18 November 1917), p. 2, cited in James Bunyan and H. H. Fisher, *The Bolshevik Revolution, 1917–1918. Documents and Materials* (Stanford, 1934), p. 221.

dinated and dispersed character of state power makes it more susceptible to the initiatives of social movements and citizens' groups, backed by countervailing networks of communication, which challenge prevailing codes and practise the art of 'divide and rule' from below.[129] Dispersed networks of communication can more easily penetrate the pores of civil society and build networks of meaning among various groups of citizens. These networks are important because they explicitly recognize the urgent need to deal with the various forms of political censorship, which have grown enormously in recent decades.

They are important for another reason: they indicate ways in which, especially among the less powerful citizenry, new forms of 'solidarity among the shaken' (Patočka) can be developed against the atomizing effects of modern life. Communicative networks can help to offset the tendency of the mass media to pile discontinuity onto us, to wash away memories, to dissolve and fast-cut, to throw away yesterday's papers.[130] De-

---

[129] See my *Democracy and Civil Society*, essay 2; and Alberto Melucci, *Nomads of the Present Social Movements and Individual Needs*, eds John Keane and Paul Mier (London, 1989). On the remarkable successes of independent citizens' media elsewhere in Europe, see H. Gordon Skilling, *Samizdat and an Independent Society in Central and Eastern Europe* (Oxford, 1989).

[130] Cf. Milan Kundera, *The Book of Laughter and Forgetting* (Harmondsworth, 1983): 'The bloody massacre in Bangladesh quickly covered over the memory of the Russian invasion of Czechoslovakia, the assassination of Allende drowned out the groans of Bangladesh, the war in the Sinai Desert made people forget Allende . . . and so on and so forth until ultimately everyone lets everything be forgotten. In times when history still moved slowly, events were few and far between and easily committed to memory. . . . Nowadays, history moves at a brisk clip (pp. 7–8).

centralized networks of communication address the dangers of 'uprootedness', and the felt need of many citizens to put down roots within civil society through forms of association which preserve particular memories of the past, a measure of stability in the present, and particular expectations for the future.[131] Finally, communications networks developed 'underneath' and 'beyond' the structures of state power – so-called bush telegraphs – have important potential for empowering citizens. They weaken the tendency (as Virginia Woolf put it) for a dozen censors to rush in, whenever we express our opinions, telling us what to say or not to say. They enable citizens to squeeze the slave out of themselves, drop by drop. They help them to cultivate the virtues of democratic citizenship: prudence, judgement, eloquence, resourcefulness, courage, self-reliance, sensitivity to power, common sense. Communications networks renew the old insight that the decentralization of power is sometimes the most effective cure for an undue parochialism; that through involvement in local organizations, citizens overcome their localism. And these networks stimulate awareness of an important new insight about power. They recognize that large-scale organizations, such as state bureaucracies and capitalist corporations, rest upon complex, molecular networks of everyday power relations – and that the strengthening and transformation of these molecular powers necessarily induces effects in these large-scale organizations.

These considerations on the decline of sovereignty lead some observers to the conclusion that the principle

---

[131] Simone Weil, *The Need for Roots. Prelude to a Declaration of Duties Towards Mankind* (London, 1952).

of seditious libel – the principle brought to bear on Paine at the end of the eighteenth century – must now be rejected as dangerous and obsolete.[132] It is argued that public discussion must never be made dependent upon government sufferance. Political freedom ends when government can use its various discretionary powers to silence its critics. The point is not the tepidly conventional liberal view that there should be room for public criticism of the government. It is rather that defamation of government is a contradiction in terms in a democracy. The right publicly to burn the national flag should be absolute, and therefore unchallengeable.

This species of libertarianism correctly spots the dangers inherent in restrictions on communications media in the name of preserving 'sovereignty'. As the leading German journalist August Ludwig von Schlözer noted prior to the French Revolution, enlightened rulers might permit wide ranging press freedom, but where freedom of the press depended on a sovereign power, it could be taken away just as easily as it was granted.[133] The deployment of the state's executive powers against dissenters in the name of 'preserving the integrity of the state' usually magnifies the attraction of anti-democratic

---

[132] See the remarks of Leonard Levy, *Emergence of a Free Press* (New York and Oxford, 1987), pp. viii–xix, and the conclusion of Zechariah Chafee Jr (*Free Speech in the United States* [Cambridge, Mass., 1942], p. 21) that the central minimum intention of the drafters and ratifiers of the First Amendment was 'to wipe out the common law of sedition, and make further prosecutions for criticism of the government, without any incitement to law-breaking, forever impossible in the United States of America'.

[133] August Ludwig von Schlözer, *Stats-Anzeigen*, vol. 8, no. 31 (1785), p. 292, cited in Franz Schneider, *Pressefreiheit und politische Öffentlichkeit* (Neuwied, 1966), p. 156.

propaganda and of authoritarian movements and parties railing against the existing order, which is itself portrayed (plausibly) as authoritarian. Besides, temporary clampdowns on the flow of opinion have a nasty habit of becoming permanent. The silencing of public criticism of political power, to borrow a phrase from Bismarck, is often the 'early fruit' (*Vorfrucht*) or precursor of more prolonged clampdowns on communication. It greatly strengthens the military and police bases of state power. It accustoms citizens to dictatorial conditions, encouraging them to turn a blind eye to disinformation and demagogy, and to act in self-serving and toadyish ways.

Libertarianism is right about all this. Yet it contains a serious blindspot. This is its failure to deal with the problem, raised in Milton's *Areopagitica*, that in matters of 'liberty of the press' the toleration of the intolerant is often a self-defeating position. The troubling fact is that freedom of communication is never a self-stabilizing process. Erskine's belief that liberty of the press guarantees civility and heals the wounds of the body politic is too sanguine. A pluralistic civil society marked by a multitude of opinions will never resemble one big happy family. It will always tend to paralyse itself. 'Visionaries and crackpots, maniacs and saints, monks and libertines, capitalists and communists and participatory democrats' (Nozick) cannot build their visions and set alluring examples without crossing each other's paths. Precisely because of its pluralism, and its lack of a guiding centre, a tongue-wagging and sign-waving, fully democratic civil society could never reach a condition of homeostasis. It would be dogged permanently by poor coordination, disagreement, niggardliness and open conflict among its constituents. Its self-critical, self-destabilizing tendencies would also make it prey to morbid attempts to put a stop to pluralism and to enforce Order. It is often true that 'conflict is a form of socialisation' (Simmel). But freedom of communication can be used to destroy freedom of communication: 'liberty of the press' gives freedom to despots and libertarians alike. The sound and fury over Islamic blasphemy and apostasy generated by Salman Rushdie's *Satanic Verses* reminds us, if the point needed accentuation, that an open and tolerant civil society can degenerate into a battlefield, in which, thanks to the existence of certain civil liberties such as 'liberty of the press', lions can roar and foxes can come to enjoy the freedom to hunt down chickens. Under extreme conditions, a quarrelling civil society can even bludgeon itself to death.[134]

That is why freedom of communication among citizens within civil society requires a vigorous *political* and *constitutional* defence. As I have argued elsewhere,[135] democratically elected and internationally coordinated parliaments are an indispensable means of aggregating, coordinating and representing diverse social interests and opinions. There is of course no guarantee that they will succeed in this. The strongest legislature cannot rise above a deeply hostile society or state. But there is no other democratic alternative. Since there is no 'natural' harmony either among social opinions or between civil society and the state, democratic parliaments are an indispensable mechanism for anticipating and alleviating the constant pressure exerted by opinionated social

---

[134] Elias, 'Violence and Civilization', in Keane, *Civil Society and the State*, pp. 177–98.

[135] See the critical remarks on Carl Schmitt's theory of sovereignty in my *Democracy and Civil Society*, essay 5.

groups upon each other, and upon the state itself. And, when faced with recalcitrant or power-hungry organizations in crises, legislatures become an indispensable – but still publicly recallable – means of ordering the arrest and punishment of those individuals who cry fire, for fun, in crowded theatres, or the suppression of those groups which worship the 'divine right of the gun' (Wole Soyinka), and which therefore consider it their duty to snarl at their 'enemies', to arm themselves to the teeth, and to destroy freedom of communication in a hail of bullets and a puff of smoke.

The Market and Civil Society

The press is free when it does not depend on either the power of government or the power of money.

Albert Camus, 1944

A second priority attends the redefinition of the public service model: the development of a plurality of *non-state* media of communication which both function as permanent thorns in the side of political power (helping thereby to minimize political censorship) and serve as the primary means of communication for citizens living, working, loving, quarrelling and tolerating others within a genuinely pluralist society.

We have seen how market liberals aim to redefine civil society and its media in the terms of commodity production and exchange guaranteed through the 'sovereign' nation–state. All media of communication are supposed to be subject to the whip of profit and loss, advertising revenues, consumer demand and threats of bankruptcy and of state censorship. Civil society is to be

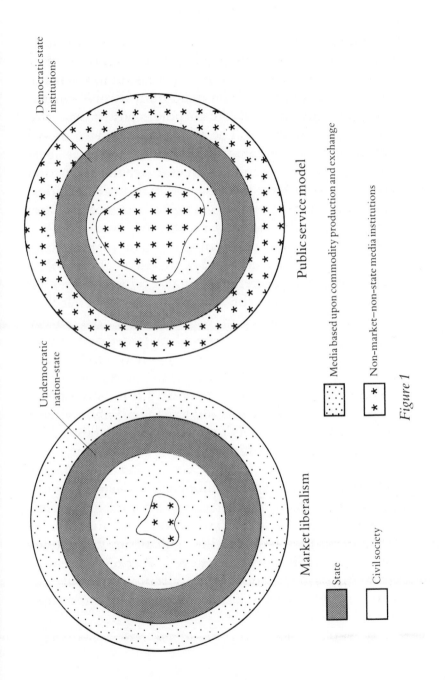

Democratic state institutions

Public service model

Undemocratic nation-state

Market liberalism

Media based upon commodity production and exchange

Non-market–non-state media institutions

State

Civil society

Figure 1

dominated by corporate speech and (when push comes
to shove) state sanctions. By contrast, a revised public
service model of communications is cast in the terms of
political democracy and the maximum feasible regulation and reduction of private corporate power over civil
society. (See figure 1.) The new public service model
admittedly shares certain features with the market liberal model of 'deregulation'. Both embrace the distinction
between civil society, the state and their intermediaries.
And both share the aim of strengthening media whose
roots are outside and underneath the state. But the
public service model parts company with market liberalism in two fundamental ways. It rejects the obsolete
doctrine of state 'sovereignty'. It also refuses to see civil
society as a synonym for 'market competition'. It tries
instead to adopt measures which protect civil society
from the self-paralysing effects of market-based media.
It implies the development of a publicly funded self-
organizing and cosmopolitan civil society which is
genuinely pluralist precisely because it is not dominated
by commodity production and exhange. Public service
media require a *post-capitalist* civil society guaranteed by
democratic state institutions.

It is unlikely, of course, that market mechanisms
structured by anonymous monetary exchanges could
ever be eliminated from the heart of a complex, pluralistic civil society. Market transactions can function as
useful accessories of social life, enhancing its produc-
tiveness, flexibility and efficiency.[136] Market-influenced
media can also function as important countervailing
forces in the process of producing and circulating

---

[136] Alec Nove, *The Economics of Feasible Socialism* (London,
1983).

opinions; they are not only economic phenomena but sites of signification that often run counter to opinion-making monopolies operated by churches and states. But, contrary to the claims of market liberalism, that does not mean that civil society and its media must be ruled by 'market forces'. There is nothing 'natural' or 'necessary' about profit-seeking, privately owned and controlled communications media. There are in fact many different types of market, whose actual designs – despite the slogan, 'Leave it to the market' – do not crystallize spontaneously. A self-regulating market is utopian, Karl Polanyi pointed out,[137] in that it cannot exist for long without paralysing itself and annulling its *social* preconditions. The actual or optimal shape of a market transaction must therefore always be crafted by political and legal regulations. It never emerges spontaneously or grows without the benefits of *non-market* support mechanisms provided by other institutions of civil society and through the state itself. And it always exists in a condition of political uncertainty, either recovering from a reform, wriggling against or cuddling up to existing regulations, or awaiting the next round of regulation.

It is difficult to be precise about which market-regulating and market-suspending strategies can maximize freedom of communication, since their actual shape and effectiveness will vary from context to context, and from time to time. One thing is nevertheless clear: the maximum feasible *decommodification* and 're-embedding' of communications media in the social life of civil society is a vital condition of freedom from state and market censorship. The recent attempts to restrict

---

[137] Karl Polanyi, *The Origins of Our Time* (London, 1945).

advertising aimed at children (in Italy) and to ban
unsolicited faxed junk mail (in the United States), and
the widening concern everywhere about sexism and
racism in the commercial media, exemplify and foresha-
dow the general principle: communications media
should not be at the whim of 'market forces', but rather
placed within a political and legal framework which
specifies tough minimum safeguards in matters of ownership structure, regional scheduling, funding, programme content and decision-making procedures.

Such public intervention in the marketplace must
avoid slipping into the reductionist demonology of the
evil media baron. The obsession with media magnates
has little in common with a politics of maximizing
freedom and equality of communication. It understates
the complexity of issues in the field of media politics and
whets old-fashioned appetites for 'nationalizing' the
media and placing them under centralized state control.
As far as possible, censorious and bureaucratic forms of
regulation should be avoided. Public intervention in the
market should be open, accountable and positively
enabling. It must use publicity to fight against the lack
of publicity. It should seek to rely upon the techniques
of 'eyebrow raising', informal and visible pressures
which encourage the media to develop programming
policies in support of decommodification. When that
fails, or is likely to fail, public regulation should aim to
entangle capitalist media in a carefully spun spider's web
of financial and legal obligations and public accountability. Public intervention in the media marketplace should
always attempt to 'level up' rather than 'level down'
citizens' non-market powers of communication.
Dogmatic presumptions in favour of one particular type
of media opinion (such as sports or current affairs

programmes) should be avoided, and it should not be forgotten that from time to time citizens can and do legitimately withdraw from the field of tension of past–present–future by relaxing and seeking small pleasures in the 'repetition, iteration, obedience to a pre-established schema' (Eco) of the mass media. Public regulation of the market should seek the creation of a genuine variety of media which enable little people in big societies to send and receive a variety of opinions. It should aim to break down media monopolies, lift restrictions upon particular audience choices and popularize the view that the media of communication are a public good, not a privately appropriable commodity whose primary function is to produce and circulate corporate speech for profit.

In practical terms, the maximization of 'liberty of the press' requries efforts to 'de-concentrate' and publicly regulate privately owned media and to restrict the scope and intensity of corporate speech. The creation of politically accountable, supra-national regulatory bodies, skilled at dealing with such matters as ownership, advertising, tariffs and network access conditions, is imperative.[138] Such bodies must be backed by national initiatives which restrict the media power of private capital by forcing such large corporations as News Corporation, Axel Springer Verlag AG and Fininvest to submit to tough legislation, which specifies programme quotas and restrictions upon advertising and cross-media ownership. Large media corporations should be treated as *common carriers*. They should be

---

[138] See Nicholas Garnham, 'European Communications Policy' (CCIS, London, October 1988).

forced by law to carry various citizens' messages, if indeed they agree to carry anyone's messages (which they must do in order to survive financially). For example, legal and financial encouragement could be given to efforts to guarantee rights of access during certain hours on radio and television to individuals, groups and independent programme makers. Such encouragement would help to build the electronic equivalent of Speakers' Corner and add a much-needed new element of spontaneous drama, fun and intellectual vitality to the media. The absolute powers of private media corporations to construct reality for others could also be broken down by the introduction of democratic decision making procedures, including experiments (such as those pioneered at *Le Monde*)[139] with worker participation and the formation of 'management teams' (*équipes de direction*).

Freedom and equality of communication also requires the drastic loosening of libel laws in favour of small producers of opinion, which find themselves unable to risk or to survive a libel claim against them by large corporations or professional bodies; libel laws should be understood less as a means of defending private reputations and more as a method of redressing inequalities of communication. It further presupposes the establishment of media enterprise boards to fund alternative ownership of divested media. 'Liberty of the press' requires public support for new media enterprises, particularly in areas (such as videotex, interactive television and electronic mail facilities) where entry costs and

---

[139] See Freiberg, *The French Press. Class, State, and Ideology*, chapter 3.

risks to potential investors are prohibitively high. It undoubtedly requires the establishment of publicly owned printing and broadcasting enterprises which utilize funds raised by an advertising revenue tax or a spectrum usage fee to facilitate new and innovative start-ups which test the market. Greater public support is needed for small production companies which operate within a regulated market and work to distinctive programming remits (as in the Channel 4 model in Britain). And, especially in the transition towards a more democratic order, freedom from state and market censorship necessitates preferential treatment of information publishers with a pluralistic cutting edge – of iconoclastic and independent media such as *El Pais* (founded a few months after Franco's death), Radio Alice (Bologna's former experimental radio station, which denied the 'reality' of reality and rejected the idea of schedules), and the courageous Czechoslovak newspaper, *Lidové Noviny*, all of which have played a critical role in the struggle for democratic rights.[140]

It is obvious that more detailed consideration must be given to the financial, legal and political feasibility of these kinds of decommodifying strategies. Late twentieth-century advocates of 'liberty of the press' must reflect hard and inventively on how best to regulate different kinds of communications market. The techniques are difficult but the principle is clear: governments committed to freedom of communication would probably want to institute a wide range of different regulated

---

[140] Juan Luis Cebrián, *The Press and Main Street: 'El Pais' – Journalism in democratic Spain* (Ann Arbor, 1990); and Umberto Eco and A. J. Grieco, 'Independent Radio in Italy: Cultural and Ideological Diversification', *Cultures*, vol. 5, no. 1 (1978), pp. 1–12.

markets for different audiences and services, whether in the fields of radio and television broadcasting, newspaper, magazine and book publishing, or satellite, mobile, aviation, maritime and point-to-point communications. In one market scheme, for example, publishing or broadcasting facilities might be leased out and eventually returned to public hands on a cyclical basis; in another, these same facilities might be sold outright, to be used either without legal restriction or subject to the regulations of a communications commission. In yet other markets, communications facilities might be sold or leased only to enterprises that operate as common carriers. And in certain broadcasting markets the mutual interference of different sets of users of the same facilities might be prevented through schemes of financial penalties.

Inevitably, stricter limits upon the production and circulation of opinions by means of market transactions would imply greater state hectoring of civil society. This is why a new constitutional settlement which ensures that political power is held permanently accountable to its citizens is so important. It is also the reason why the undermining of both arcane state power and market power requires the development of a dense network or 'heterarchy' of communications media which are controlled *neither by the state nor by commercial markets*. Publicly funded, non-profit and legally guaranteed media institutions of civil society, some of them run voluntarily and held directly accountable to their audiences through democratic procedures, are an essential ingredient of a revised public service model. Numerous examples come to mind. The BBC model of broadcasting institutions, funded by a licence fee, could remain a leading symbol of the non-market–non-state sector, but only at the price of the abolition of the present system of government appointment of its management, the acknowledgement that its original (Reithian) brief is not fully attainable, and its internal democratization (perhaps along the lines of the system adopted in the Federal Republic of Germany, where representatives of 'socially relevant groups', including political parties, have exercised some measure of influence over such matters as programming schedules, personal budgets and organizational structure and where there have been tentative efforts to develop public access or open radio and television channels [Offene Kanäle]). Other examples of this sector include the development of local independent cinemas and recording studios, networks of media training institutions and leased-back broadcasting facilities. Political newspapers could be publicly subsidized. A dense and user-friendly network of community libraries equipped with the latest information technologies could be strengthened. Cooperatively run publishers and distributors, community radio stations and other conventional non-profit media would continue to play an important role in strengthening the foundations of a pluralist civil society. More versatile interpersonal communication could be ensured through publicly funded and equitably distributed telefaxes, videotex systems and electronic mail facilities. The development of publicly funded teleshopping facilities, which are most useful to housebound and senior citizens, would also have priority. And support could be provided for the development of new types of equipment – interactive televisions, digital copiers, camcorders and music synthesizers – capable of supporting the communication of opinions among various groups of citizens.

As far as possible, these non–market–non–state media would feed upon the increased flexibility and power and reduced costs of information processing provided by the new microelectronic technologies. Consider the small press. The ready availability of increasingly affordable computer technology makes possible strengthened and financially viable small publishing houses. The tasks computers can perform for them are virtually endless: editing, spelling correction, typesetting, indexing, accounting and networking among authors, wholesalers, distributors, booksellers and buyers are but a few.[141] Such benefits are not confined to small book publishing. The new digital technologies, as market liberals have been quick to point out, have profound implications for a revised public service model. They are revolutionary heartland technologies, whose cost-reducing effects and ever-widening applicability throughout civil society and the state enable citizens to communicate in previously unthinkable ways. They are potentially a species of 'democratic technics' (Mumford).

Improvements in their performance are not yet complete. Optical-fibre channel capacity, software quality, random access memory (RAM) capacity, chip density and processing speeds continue to undergo rapid improvement. Nevertheless, these technologies have several unique characteristics in common. They treat all kinds of information (speech, text, video, graphics) in digital form, thus facilitating the transfer of the same data between different media. The new technologies decrease the relative cost of information processing;

---

[141] William M. Brinton, *Publishing in a Global Village: A Role for the Small Press* (San Francisco, 1987).

bulk operations that would previously have been un-thinkable can now be carried out. The decreasing size of equipment and the speedier information processing and error-checking capacities also enable smaller-scale, de-centralized and user-friendly operations within a framework of greater coordination and strategic control which links operations over vast distances. And – this feature is crucial – the new information technologies rupture the traditional television and radio pattern of offering a continuous sequence of programmes to mass audiences. Instead, the new electronic services streng-then the hand of 'narrowcasting' against broadcasting. They offer information on a more individualized basis: at any given moment, the 'receiver' is required to choose or to process the specific information she or he wants.[142]

At the same time, paradoxically, the microelectronic technologies tend to 'socialize' certain means of communication.[143] They reinforce the principle, lam-pooned by market liberals but so essential to a revised public service model, that the means of communication belong to the public at large. The new technologies strengthen the tendency whereby the element of rights to dispose of property privately becomes obsolete in the communications field. It has always been difficult to define property rights in the broadcast media. Those holding rights to occupy a plot of land or to mine the gold or uranium beneath its surface can establish pre-cisely the dimensions of their claims. By contrast,

---

[142] Ian Miles, *Information Technology and Information Society: Options for the Future* (Brighton, 1988).

[143] G. J. Mulgan, *Rethinking Freedom in the Age of Digital Networks* (CCIS, London, October 1988); John Chesterman and Andy Lipman, *The Electronic Pirates* (London, 1988).

broadcast frequencies are intangibles ('ether') that become meaningful as property only in conjunction with the technical means of transmission and reception. A similar problem of definition is evident in the justified treatment of postal systems and telephone networks as common carriers of signals. In microelectronic technologies, producers of information are also finding it difficult to keep their 'products' scarce and exclusive. They invoke copyright laws, frustrate attempts to copy data, scramble signals and mount other rearguard actions. But information is widely reproduced, transmitted, sampled and reconfigured without permission. In the United States, where 'theft' of satellite television signals was to be prevented by scrambling them with the allegedly foolproof VCII system, it is estimated that half of the descramblers are now used illegally, adjusted to bypass the transmitters' controls.

Such practices challenge the principle of privately controlled means of communication. Communication comes to be seen as *flows* among publics rather than as an exchange among discrete commodities which can be owned and controlled privately as things. This trend is arguably strengthened by the high capacity digital networks (such as ISDN) currently being planned and constructed in Japan, Europe, the United States and elsewhere. These networks enable individuals and groups to transmit 'private' messages to others through a common network, subject only to covering the cost of the transmission, which in any case could be reduced by treating the networks as a public facility, rather than as a source of private profit.

Democracy, Risks and Reversals

He who first shortened the labour of copyists by device of
Movable Types *was disbanding hired armies, and cashiering*
most Kings and Senates, and creating a whole new democratic
world: he had invented the art of printing.

Thomas Carlyle, 1836

In practice, these priorities – a new constitutional settlement, state regulation and restriction of private media markets and the development of a plurality of non-market, non-state communications systems – would radically alter the prevailing definition of the public service model, without capitulating to the charms of market liberalism. Public service communications would henceforth refer to the whole infrastructure of state-funded and state-protected and non-state institutions of communication which serve to circulate opinions among a wide plurality of citizens. Among the key advantages of the revised public service model sketched here is its theoretical and practical recognition of complexity. Moving out from under the shadow of Lord Reith, it recognizes that 'freedom of communication' comprises a bundle of (potentially) conflicting component freedoms. It acknowledges that in a complex society the original public service assumption that all the citizens of a nation-state can talk to each other like a family sitting and chatting around the domestic hearth is unworkable; that it is impossible for all citizens simultaneously to be full-time senders and receivers of information; that at any point in time and space some citizens will normally choose to remain silent and only certain other individuals and groups will choose to communicate with others; and that (as the famous Red Lion decision of the United States Supreme Court affirmed)[144] this freedom publicly to express or receive opinions is not identical with the freedom to own and control the means of communication.

The public service model defended in this essay does justice to these elementary principles of free and equal communication. It acknowledges the existence of an ineradicably modern dilemma between the universalist goal of empowering *all citizens* through mechanisms which *enable* them to express their opinions *collectively* and the pluralist goal of securing a genuine variety of opinions through mechanisms which clear spaces for *particular* citizens to express their opinions by *checking* and *restricting* the power of expression of other citizens, who are thereby consigned to the role of passive *audiences*. It thus rejects the (early modern) belief in the possibility of communicational abundance, in which every tool of the media is a genuine means of lateral communication (a part in a 'huge linked system . . . capable not only of transmitting but receiving', in the words of Bertolt Brecht), and every receiver of opinions is also a sender of opinions. The public service model rejects this myth of transparent communication. It is instead based on the assumption that the alternative to inequalities of communicative freedom is not the elimination of forms of media representation but the proliferation of a wide variety of countervailing media,

---

[144] *Red Lion Broadcasting* v. *FCC*, 395 US 367, 23 L. ed. 2d. 371, 89 8, Ct. 1794 (1969).

only some of which are subject to the time-consuming and unwieldy procedures of 'direct democracy'.

As well, the new public service model sketched here is well suited to face up to the facts of social diversity – the differences between regions, country and city, young and old, rich and poor and groupings based on occupation, ethnic identify, language, gender and sexual preference – which are ever more characteristic of the United States, Canada, France, Britain and other west European countries. The revised public service model consequently avoids the reductionism of monistic accounts of contemporary media. Guided by the distinction between the institutions of the state, those of civil society and their intermediaries, it emphasizes that existing communication systems interact in complex ways with other social and political institutions. Much critical research and commentary on mass communications ignores these bothersome complexities. It views existing state power as the central impediment to 'freedom of choice and information' (as in the market liberal polemic); or it draws upon the equally suspect hypothesis that 'the mass media contribute to ideological relations in capitalist society by participating in the reproduction of basic and pervasive *class divisions*';[145] or it openly champions the 'independent' sector of communications – small, non-profit and user-friendly publishing houses, film co-ops, community radio stations – which are viewed as the normative standard for all other types of communications medium.

The 'mixed' model of communications proposed here defies these three forms of reductionism. And by acknowledging the normative and empirical complexity of

---

[145] Freiberg, *The French Press. Class, State, and Ideology*, p. 14.

things, it no longer bases itself – as the classical defences of 'liberty of the press' did – upon supposedly absolute principles, such as God, natural rights, the utility principle, Truth or (in its early twentieth-century version) Reith. The new public service model avoids the pitfalls of foundationalist reasoning. It rejects the claim that this model 'presupposes' a doctrine about the nature of human beings. It doubts the reasoning (but not the fine intentions) of such philosophical claims as 'liberty of speech, conviction and information figure among *fundamental* human rights' (Dworkin). It denies the need for an account of 'a good in common' and of 'the nature of the moral subject' which is 'necessary, non-contingent and prior to any particular experience' (Sandel). It is instead guided, philosophically speaking, by a form of democratic scepticism which acknowledges the facts of complexity, diversity and difference, and – in plain English – harbours doubts about whether any one person, group, committee, party or organization can ever be trusted to make superior choices on matters of concern to citizens. The new public service model embraces the insight of the Czech humorist Jan Werich, who observed that the struggle against the stupidity of those who exercise power is the only human struggle that is always in vain, but can never be abandoned. In sum, the public service model is best seen as a vital requirement of an open, tolerant and lively society in which great big dogmas and smelly little orthodoxies of all kinds are held in check, and in which, thanks to the existence of a genuine plurality of media of communication, various individuals and groups can openly express their solidarity with (or their opposition to) other citizens' likes and dislikes, proposals, tastes and ideals.

Fundamental questions to do with democracy arise at this point: would a revivified and expanded public service model serve to reinforce conventional wisdom about democracy? Might it force a radical change in our understanding of its principles and procedures? Could it deepen our appreciation of its positive advantages – and its limitations?

Clear-headed responses to such questions are important, if only because the concept of democracy is presently dogged by confusion. What exactly does democracy mean in this context? The concept of democracy is not infinitely elastic, even though its principles have been interpreted in diverse ways, as their custodianship has changed hands. The struggle to control the definition of democracy is an intrinsic feature of modern societies. And yet democracy is not a word which can be made to mean whatever we choose it to mean. Democracy is best understood as a system of procedural rules with normative implications. These rules specify *who* is authorized to make collective decisions and through which *procedures* such decisions are to be made, regardless of the areas of life in which democracy is practised. In contrast to all forms of heteronomous government, democracy comprises procedures for arriving at collective decisions in a way which secures the fullest possible and qualitatively best participation of interested parties. At a minimum – here the normative implications of my proceduralist definition of democracy become evident – democratic procedures include equal and universal adult suffrage; majority rule and guarantees of minority rights, which ensure that collective decisions are approved by a substantial number of those entitled to make them; the rule of law; and constitutional guarantees of freedom of assembly and expression and other liberties, which help ensure that the people expected to decide or to elect those who decide can choose among real alternatives. Representative mechanisms are a necessary condition of democratic procedures. In large-scale, complex societies, regular assemblies of 'the people' as a whole are technically impossible. Direct democracy, the participation of citizens in the *agora*, is suited only to small states and organizations in which 'the people find it easy to meet and in which every citizen can easily get to know all the others' (Rousseau). That is why modern democracy requires both mechanisms of representation and the institutional division of state and civil society, that is, the building of a pluralistic, self-organizing (international) civil society which is coordinated and guaranteed by multilayered (supra-national) state institutions, which are in turn held permanently accountable to civil society by mechanisms – political parties, legislatures, communications media – which keep open the channels between state and social institutions.[146]

This revised understanding of democracy does not imply that representative, parliamentary democracy is the alpha and omega of political forms. In Western countries, the representative system is in need of drastic repairs. It is besieged by various undemocratic trends, such as the decline of legislatures and the growth of secretive military and policing agencies and other forms of state censorship. It is also constrained and limited by accumulations of *social* power within civil society. The vast majority of citizens has no say in major decisions

---

[146] This theme is developed in my *Public Life and Late Capitalism*; and my *Democracy and Civil Society*.

concerning economic investment, production, growth and environmental impact. Churches, households, trade unions, media and many other institutions of civil society remain insufficiently democratic. This suggests the need to refine and extend democracy by broadening the domains where citizens can live in accordance with the minimal requirements of democracy. Exactly how more democracy within the sphere of civil society might be achieved in practice is a central theme of my *Democracy and Civil Society*. It argues for the extension of the process of democratization from the political sphere (where individuals are regarded as citizens of a state) to the civil sphere, where there are multiple and conflicting identities, where individuals are regarded variously as men and women, entrepreneurs and work-ers, teachers and students, speakers and listeners, pro-ducers and consumers. Struggles over *where* citizens can vote should be given as much priority as the struggles in the nineteenth and early twentieth centuries over *who* can vote.

'But what is so good about democracy, aside from the fact that most people today say it's a good thing?', our critic asks. 'Why sympathize with the democratic method – especially considering the fact that in the history of political thought democracy has had many more enemies than friends?'

Such questions exploit democracy's lack of philo-sophical self-confidence. They need to be answered. In a famous aphorism, Novalis pointed out that philosophy *qua* philosophy is required to explain itself. This aphor-ism applies equally to contemporary democratic theory, which is slowly waking from an extended period of inebriated merrymaking. Despite their current popular-ity, democratic ideals nowadays resemble a homeless drunk staggering uncertainly in search of a lamp-post for support, if not illumination. This was not always so. For the past two centuries democratic thinkers in Europe and elsewhere have attempted to justify democracy by referring back to a substantive grounding principle. There are many cases that can be cited: the belief of Mazzini and others that the growth of democracy is a Law of History; the argument of Tom Paine, Georg Forster and others that it is grounded in the natural rights of citizens; the Benthamite assumption that democracy is an implied condition of the principle of utility; the conviction of Theodor Parker and others that it is a form of government based on the principle of eternal justice, on the unchanging law of God; and the (Marxian) claim that the triumph of authentic democracy is dependent upon the world-historical struggle of the proletariat. Belief in these various first principles has today crumbled, and that is why democracy is no longer understandable as a self-evidently desirable set of procedural norms. Democracy is now suffering a deep crisis of legitimacy. Philosophical insecurity is the quintessential feature of the contemporary democratic identity, which consequently feels embarrassed and vulnerable before its fundamentalist critics, who preach the teachings of Allah, or advocate the Rule of Law, the sactity of the Nation or some other substantive principle.

Can this insecurity be tempered, if not overcome? In *Public Life and Late Capitalism* I argued (against Habermas and others) that democracy should not be treated as a form of life guided by substantive normative principles. I questioned the view, associated with various forms of 'Socratism' (Kierkegaard), that argumentative reason can separate truth and falsity and produce a consensus among speaking and interacting subjects. Following a clue provided in Hans Kelsen's *Vom Wesen und Wert der Demokratie*,[147] I proposed that the philosophy of democracy cannot become a universal language game, capable of knowing everything, refuting all its opponents and pointing to the practical synthesis of all differences. I further proposed that democracy can survive and thrive without philosophical presuppositions, that it is best understood as an implied condition and practical consequence of the recognition that our modern world is marked (however imperfectly) by trends towards philosophical and political pluralism. The argument foregrounded the (potentially) irreducible plurality of language games in contemporary societies. It did not suppose itself to be a privileged language game. I proposed that a philosophy of democracy can cover itself against this self-contradiction by relying on the logic of occasion first developed by the Greek sophists. The key feature of this logic of argument is its rejection of claims in support of one universal truth by highlighting the ways in which both itself and its opponents' claims are only individual cases of the logic of the special case, of the particular or unique occasion. I concluded from these reflections that the separation of civil society from the state, as well as the democratization of each – a post-capitalist civil society guarded by a democratic political system – are necessary conditions for enabling a genuine plurality of individuals and groups openly to express their solidarity with (or opposition to) others' ideals and forms of life,

---

[147] Hans Kelsen, *Vom Wesen und Wert der Demokratie* (Tübingen, 1981 [1929]), pp. 98–104; and his 'Foundations of Democracy', *Ethics*, vol. 66 (October 1955), pp. 1–101.

and even to dispute the principles and practice of 'democracy' and 'freedom of communication' as such.

Understood in this new way, the concept of democratization joins hands with a revised model of public service media. Each requires the other, if only to underscore its abandonment of the futile search for transhistorical ideals, definite Truths and safe highroads of human existence. Each rejects the pre-political wistfulness of philosophical and ethical 'relativism', with its smug conclusion that everything is just a matter of 'preference'. Each refuses the guilt-ridden pseudopluralism of those who conclude, inconsistently, that democracy and freedom of communication are mere ideals of our western civilization. Each is driven by a profound scepticism and mistrust of Power and Ideals in *every* civilization. Together, they make it more possible for all citizens of the earth to live without dogmas, including the indefensible ideological claims – Order, Progress, Truth, History, Humanity, Nature, Socialism, Individualism, Utility, Nation, Sovereignty of the People – upon which the early modern advocates of democracy and 'liberty of the press' based their case for greater equality and freedom.

Risks and Reversals

Ever tried. Ever failed. No matter. Try again. Fail again. Fail better.

Samuel Beckett, 1961

This non-foundationalist understanding of democracy and public service media requires considerable elaboration. It certainly needs to extend the frontiers of the

contemporary imagination by providing new and undogmatic arguments for the compatibility and superiority of both the democratic method and public service
communications. Consider just one example from the
field of environmental policy.

Anxiety about the effects of environmental waste and
degradation on human life in the next century is everywhere growing. There are justified fears that certain key
resources will be depleted, that toxic wastes will affect
our health and that climatic changes may occur. Indeed,
both the scale and complexity of these ecological problems and the difficult task of shifting to sustainable
patterns of growth confront us with massive *risks*.[148]
The production and distribution of environmental risks,
in the sense of probable hazards to human life resulting
from our exposure to certain substances and ecosyste-
mic changes, is now for the first time becoming prob-
lematic on a global scale. The harmful risks generated
by water pollution, radiation and greenhouse effects
have levelling effects upon us. They are neither geog-
raphically nor sociologically limited; they criss-cross
national boundaries and boomerang on rich and poor,
the powerful and the less powerful alike. They tend to
devalue the economic and aesthetic value of property (as
the death of forests shows). And many of the new
environmental risks – from poisonous additives in
foodstuffs to nuclear and chemical contaminants – are
'invisible'; they elude human perception and, in certain
cases, their effects are detectable only in the offspring of
those who are currently affected. The growing quantity

---

[148] Ulrich Beck, *Risikogesellschaft – Auf den Weg in eine andere
Moderne* (Frankfurt, 1986); and the same author's *Gegengifte –
Die organisierte Unverantwortlichkeit* (Frankfurt, 1989).

of these environmental risks suggests that we are in the midst of a massive, long-term experiment with ourselves and our biospheric environment. Our productive powers are as awesome as the obligation to exercise these powers prudently.

Under pressure from these unprecedented environmental risks, democratic procedures – backed up by public service media which serve as early warning devices that circulate new and controversial opinions about such risks – have a revivified and wholly novel pertinence. In the past, the close relationship between democracy and the media has been justified in various ways. We have considered, for instance, the utilitarian claim that democratic mechanisms and a free press guarantee that the best interpreters of interests – the interested parties themselves – can sift through various options and decide for themselves. Others have insisted that democracy and an independent media are justified by their ability to maximize freedom in the sense of individual or group autonomy. Still others have viewed democracy and a free press as superior because they are the strongest antidote to the abuse of power. In the face of the new risks, each of these conventional arguments appears flawed. The early modern thesis that freedom of communication is a vehicle for certitude, absolute knowledge and the spread of a rational democratic consensus is obsolete. New justifications of the intimate relationship between 'liberty of the press' and democracy are needed.

The risk-based argument sketched here promises one such justification. It cuts across the grain of the conventional thesis that the most important quality of freedom of information and democratic procedures is that they enable the approval of decisions of interest to the whole collectivity, or at least to a majority of citizens. The point has become something of a cliché. Democracy requires informed citizens. Their capacity to produce intelligent agreements by democratic means can be nurtured only when they enjoy equal and open access to diverse sources of opinion. The idea has early modern roots, for instance, in the writings of James Madison: 'A popular Government, without popular information, or the means of acquiring it, is but a Prologue to a Farce or a Tragedy; or, perhaps both. Knowledge will forever govern ignorance: And a people who mean to be their own Governors, must arm themselves with the power which knowledge gives.'[149]

This early modern argument overlooks the key point – still inadequately recognized in democratic theory and media studies – that democratic procedures and public sevice media also facilitate *disagreement*. They enable the *disapproval* and *revision* of established agreements, and for this reason they are uniquely suited to complex societies beset with ecological problems. A plurality of uncensored media could break down the present pattern of simplified and prejudiced media reporting of risks. Media coverage of risks today often apes the point of view of governments, corporations and professional information czars. Insufficient attention is given to the opinions of dissident scientists and to events not pre-packaged for audience consumption. General assignment and local-beat reporters and their editors are often ill-informed about the complexity of risk situations. Risks tend to be treated as isolated and sensational novelties. They are neither situated in wider socio-

---

[149] James Madison, 'Letter to W. T. Barry (4 August 1822)', in *The Writings of James Madison*, vol 9, p. 103.

technical contexts nor placed in the perspective of alternative or competing risks. They are reduced to the status of 'accidents' and 'calamities', along with tornadoes, mid-air collisions, chemical plant fires and gas explosions.[150]

A public service system of communications would be likely to democratize these patterns of risk definition. It would reduce the quantity of prejudiced and sensationalist media reporting of hazards, the premature disclosure of poorly analysed information, and oversimplifications and distortions in interpreting technical risk information. It could help to expose the hidden socioeconomic and political powers working self-interestedly to manage the public definition of risks. It could heighten awareness of the deep uncertainties in risk estimation and management. Public service media could thereby stimulate the public acceptance of level-headed strategies for reducing or eliminating serious risks.

In these tasks public service media would undoubtedly be aided by more and better democracy in the institutions of civil society and the state. Democratic procedures are superior to all other types of decision making, not because they guarantee both a consensus and 'good' decisions, but because they provide citizens who are affected by certain decisions with the possibility

---

[150] See Nancy Pfund and Laura Hofstadter, 'Biomedical Innovation and the Press', *Journal of Communication*, vol. 31, no. 2 (1981), pp. 138–54; David B. Sachsman et al., 'Improving Press Coverage of Environmental Risk', *Industrial Crisis Quarterly*, vol. 2, no. 3–4 (1989), pp. 283–96; and Eleanor Singer and Phyllis Endreny, 'Reporting Hazards: Their Benefits and Costs', *Journal of Communication*, vol. 37, no. 3 (Summer 1987), pp. 10–26.

of *reconsidering* their judgements about the quality and unintended consequences of these decisions. Democratic procedures sometimes allow the majority to decide things about which they are blissfully ignorant; but they also enable minorities to challenge blissfully ignorant majorities, to bring them to their senses. They enable some citizens to tell others what they do not want to hear. Democratic procedures enable citizens to think twice and to say no. They even heighten their awareness that there is a hierarchy of decisions, and that certain decisions, once implemented, may be *irreversible*. Democratic procedures are for this reason best suited to the task of publicly monitoring and controlling (and sometimes shutting down) complex and tightly coupled 'high-risk' organizations, whose failure (as in Bhopal, Three Mile Island, Chernobyl and Ust-Kamenogorsk) can have catastrophic ecological and social consequences. Max Weber once defined democracy, for General Ludendorff's benefit (and with his approval), as a system in which 'the people choose a leader who then says, "Now shut up and obey me".' Such impatience with disagreement and the clash of opinions misses the key advantage of democracy. Democratic procedures increase the level of flexibility and reversibility – or 'biodegradability' – of decision making. They invite dispute. They create dissatisfaction with conditions as they are, and even stir citizens to anger. And they recognize the inescapable need in social and political life to resort to solomonic judgements (Elster). In the face of uncertainty about how to cope with our own ignorance, democratic procedures encourage incremental learning and trial-and-error modification, or 'muddling through'. Decisions are based on revocable preferences which are, in turn, the resultant of deliberate and considered confrontations among at least several competing points of view.

Only democratic procedures, reinforced by a plurality of communications media, can openly and fairly select certain kinds of danger for public attention, and carefully monitor and bring to heel those responsible for managing risky organizations, thereby minimizing the possibility of error and reducing the chances of the big mistake. Democratic procedures and public service media are in this respect essential correctives to the wishful (Hayekian) belief in the decentralized anonymity of the market as a superior self-correcting mechanism in a world of complex pressures and interconnections. They are also important correctives to the mistaken trust in the therapeutic powers of unbridled technical expertise. Unchecked technocratic power, with its belief in the omnipotence and beneficence of scientific–technical progress, has been partly responsible for the rising incidence and severity of ecological damage. Current attempts by professional experts to monopolize the process of defining and reducing risks are therefore as implausible as the claim to infallibility of a Pope who has recently converted to Protestantism. The belief in technocratic solutions remains wedded to outdated empiricist assumptions about the nature of science and fails to come to terms with the decidedly *chaotic* fluctuations within the ecosystem.[151] It conveniently

---

[151] Ian Stewart, *Does God Play Dice?* (Harmondsworth, 1990). On the overturning of many established ideas on coherence and stability in the field of radiation physics, see the introductory remarks in F. T. Arecchi and R. G. Harrison (eds), *Instabilities and Chaos in Quantum Optics* (London, Paris, Tokyo, 1988); and Tito Arecchi, 'Chaos and Complexity', *Liber*, vol. 1 (October 1989), pp. 16–17.

ignores the current lack of consensus on some basic terms, including the term 'risk' itself. It does not properly acknowledge that the language games used to define and portray risk frame the policy process, and in turn govern the attempted regulation of risk.[152] In relying upon risk assessment and risk management techniques, the belief in technocratic solutions also understates the extent to which ongoing *judgements* are inescapable in the complex process of identifying, ranking and regulating the bewildering array of potential hazards and their possible health and environmental risks. The belief in technocratic solutions is also dangerous insofar as it can bolster the temptation to deal with environmental risks through *dirigiste* policies or by resorting to states of emergency and crackdowns on the media.

Democracy and public service media are unrivalled remedies for technocratic delusions of this kind. They raise the level and quality of 'risk communication'[153] by

---

[152] Compare the introductory remarks of Dorothy Nelkin, in Dorothy Nelkin (ed.), *The Language of Risk* (Beverly Hills, 1985), p. 21: 'The choice of language, a reflection of values, also is a strategic choice, for language carries implications for the formulation of policy. For example, if the problems of risk are defined in terms of insufficient technical evidence, this implies that "risk assessment", with all its connotations of objectivity and neutrality, is the appropriate approach to regulation, and that regulation is properly the province of expertise. If the problems are defined in the social or moral context of responsibility or justice, this calls for more political approaches to public policy. In this way, the discourse frames the policy agenda.'

[153] J. C. Davies et al. (eds), *Risk Communication* (Washington, DC, 1987); and Vince Covello et al., 'Risk Communication: A Review of the Literature', *Risk Abstracts*, vol. 3 (1986), pp. 171–82.

guaranteeing the open flow of opinions, risk evaluations and controversies back and forth among individual citizens, academic experts, administrators, interest groups and social movements. Democratic procedures combined with public service media can open up and render accountable the process in which citizens, experts and policymakers comprehend, estimate, evaluate and deal with the probabilities and consequences of risks. They are an indispensable means of rendering accountable those politicians and entrepreneurs who turn a blind eye to the environmental damage and 'normal accidents' (Perrow) which plague high-risk projects. They are a vital means of breaking down unwarranted confidence in 'the facts'. They help ensure that risk data are expressed in publicly understandable terms, that the profound uncertainties surrounding risk estimates are widely appreciated, and that the intuitive sense of risk among citizens is acknowledged and respected, not dismissed as 'irrational nonsense'. Public service media and democratic procedures are also vital methods of controlling professional experts who seek to define acceptable levels of risk by means of technical analyses of probability – or simply by falling back on the childish solipsism that whatever is not believed could not possibly be harmful.

Democracy and public service media are reflexive means of controlling the exercise of power. They are unsurpassed methods of checking the unending arrogance and foolishness of those who wield it. Contrary to the view of conservatives, who blindly trust in the unadventurous prudence of the anointed few, they are the best friends of practical wisdom. Democracy and public service media are unparalleled early warning devices. They help to define and publicize risks that are not worth taking. They dampen the reckless impulse to sail uncharted oceans, to risk getting lost or shipwrecked. They ensure that a known good is not lightly surrendered for an unknown better. They navigate the rough seas of uncertainty with caution and prudence.

Information Blizzards

Eveything is destined to reappear as simulation. Landscapes as photography, women as the sexual scenario, thoughts as writing, terrorism as fashion and the media, events as television. Things seem only to exist by virtue of this strange destiny. You wonder whether the world itself isn't just here to serve as advertising copy in some other world.

Jean Baudrillard, 1986

This essay has presented only a crude summary of a complex theoretical and political controversy about the media and democracy. Its proposals for securing public service media against market liberalism, in whose hands liberty and equality are unsafe, are undoubtedly in need of refinement and development. No model legislation or budget or detailed political strategy has been provided. The nitty-gritty economic and organizational details so necessary for successfully rebuilding and extending the public service model have been understated. And so far no consideration has been given to the new dangers harboured in the communications model sketched here. Consider the following example.

In the early modern period, it was widely assumed that citizens were threatened by a *scarcity* of information, and that using the press to cast stones of critical opinion at the windows of secretive power would cause a public sensation. Despotic power would be shattered. Citizens would see the world clearly governing themselves in broad daylight, without deception and misunderstanding. Today, with rare exceptions, the opposite trend is dominant. The world seems so full of information that what is scarce is citizens' capacities to make sense of it. The release of new opinions through the media rarely shatters unaccountable power. Publicity better resembles the throwing of snowballs into a blizzard – or the blowing of bubbles into warm summer's air. Our systems are 'high density information societies' (Melucci). Each month Hollywood is showered by 25,000 unsolicited scripts and treatments of subjects stretching from murdered aerobic instructors to playing golf with Jesus.[154] Each year in Britain 50,000 new books are published. Each day Americans are exposed on average to some 1,600 commercial advertisements. By the mid-1990s it is anticipated that Europe will have satellite capacity for at least 250 television channels.

A fully democratic system of communications could exacerbate the trend symbolized by these examples. It could produce information overload – the swamping of citizens by a bewildering set of dials and electronic gadgets, scores of alternative radio and television programmes, hundreds of magazines and journals, thousands of flyers, electronic leaflets and manuscripts, and millions of books. There are indeed dangers – highlighted in the recent analyses by Jean Baudrillard – that citizens will become trapped in a never-ending blizzard of information, without adequate free time to digest or make sense of the information flows which envelop them.

---

[154] Larry Rohter, 'A Supermarket of Scripts, in Paperback', *New York Times* (4 September 1990), pp. B1, B5.

Consider Baudrillard's *L'Autre par lui-même* (1987).[155] This essay proposes that we live in a modern universe of hyper-communication which plunges citizens into an all-embracing vortex of coded messages. Every sphere of life becomes a potential grazing ground of the media. The universe is transformed into a giant monitoring screen. All publicity serves as an apology for publicity. Information ceases to be linked to events, but becomes a gripping event in itself. Citizens are entombed within images that are set free; the world is so saturated with a sense of hyper-reality that citizens are no longer capable of knowing what they want. In spite of themselves, they become schizophrenic: open to everything and permanently bewildered. They are reduced to 'masses' capable (at best) of acting as recalcitrant children uttering 'yes' or 'no'.

Baudrillard's work reminds us that the powerful always aim to monopolize graphic space by visibly marking the land, buildings, streets, people and customs which they seek to control. It also provides a healthy antidote to the cavalier confidence in native public scepticism ('everybody knows how bad the media really are'). Yet the dangers of an information blizzard should not be exaggerated (as they are by Baudrillard). Democrats are not required to cancel their newspaper deliveries, to unplug their personal computers or to smash up their television sets. The power of the mass communications media to mould our lives is limited; despite their deeply manipulative character, they are fated to remain media of *communication* and *controversy*.

---

[155] Jean Baudrillard, *L'Autre par lui-Même* (Paris, 1987). Similar themes are developed in his *Amérique* (Paris, 1986) and *The Evil Demon of Images* (Sydney, 1988).

For a start, there are signs of increasing restiveness in western democracies about the loss of personal 'privacy' due to the privileges accorded broadcasters and print journalists. There is a growing sense that the reporter's great story is sometimes the victim's disastrous fire (to recall another remark of A. J. Liebling). In the United States, for example, controversies have erupted over such matters as reporters' access to public facilities (as in the attempt of a San Francisco television station, KQED, to film inside a prison)[156] and broadcasters' invasion of personal privacy (by divulging from official court records the name of a woman who had been raped).[157] The dangers of a permanent information blizzard are also offset by unpredictable audience reactions. The significance of opinions transmitted through the media is generated at the interface between a medium and its users. This interface is the site of transformation of the message, the medium and the user. The medium is never simply the message. Fiske and others have exaggerated this point, but the trends are clear. There are perceived time constraints upon audiences. A great achievement of the newspaper was that it circulated rapidly decaying opinions and, hence, the need to reconsume fresh opinions. This power of the media to manipulate citizens' time arguably declines under conditions of information swamping, since the time available to citizens to consume information is

---

[156] *Houchins* v. *KQED, Inc.*, 438 US 1 (1978).

[157] *Cox Broadcasting Corp.* v. *Cohn*, 420 US 469 (1975). In *Nixon* v. *Warner Communications, Inc.*, 435 US 589, 608–9 (1978), this case was said to involve the 'right of access of the press'. See also Larry Gross et al. (eds), *Image Ethics: The Moral Rights of Subjects in Photographs, Film, and Television* (New York, 1988).

physically limited. A growing proportion of information is never received, let alone interpreted.

There is evidence, for example, that the proliferation of market-led 'choice' may have the ironic effect of weakening the legendary power of television. The growth in the number of channels (and videos) tends to rupture and overwhelm viewing habits by introducing a surge of unfamiliar programmes. Lacking simple solutions, at least some viewers resort to avoidance. They develop an aversion to 'evenings stuck in front of the box'. Especially when programme types and themes are provided in triplicate or quadruplicate, widespread boredom sets in. The vast repertoire of television opportunities results (according to Howard Stringer, president of the American CBS network) in a 'vast, media-jaded audience that wanders restlessly from one channel to another in search of that endangered species – originality'.[158]

The remarkable growth of photocopying, computer hacking and video piracy also suggests that today many citizens retain a native (if underdeveloped) capacity to reduce the complexity of information flows to manageable proportions, to select, criticize, reinterpret or – like tortoises – shield themselves completely against flows of information. Some individuals and groups of citizens even conduct 'semiotic guerrilla warfare' (Eco) by using photocopiers, telephones and computers to wound corporate media and their dominating images of reality. In addition, many citizens are at least vaguely aware that the media are engaged in story-building and story-

---

[158] Quoted from his address to the Royal Television Society, 'Free Market Fairy Tales and the Pursuit of Quality Television' (London, 4 April 1990).

telling activities guided by stocks of recipe knowledge, institutional routines and technical tricks ranging from various kinds of staging to newsroom categories such as 'scoops' and 'second-day leads'. It is therefore not surprising that there is a strong tendency for citizens to attend to the messages and stories with which they already identify. They perceive mainly those features of ambiguous or complex stories that fit in with their perceived tastes. They tend to rely on trusted friends and relatives to develop their opinions about the world.

Those alarmed by the possibility of information blizzards also forget that a new public service model could help reinforce a culture of freedom of communication. Consider book publishing. George Steiner and others have proposed that the 'age of the book', spanning the period from the 1550s to the 1950s, is now gradually coming to an end.[159] That period experienced the rapid decline of the medieval chained library and the practice of holding books as treasures in certain monastic and princely institutions. Books became domestic objects owned by their users, accessible at their will for reading and re-reading in a circle of silence. Readers could concentrate on texts. They could quote them at length and discuss them with magisterial seriousness. Publishers, authors and readers fashioned a public echo chamber of serious ideas and controversial themes. Today, it is claimed, citizens become cocooned in a world cluttered with signs and noise. Personal libraries become rare. Bookishness withers away. Bookworms become social isolates. Attention spans decline. Readers flip through glossy magazines and cheap paperbacks

---

[159] George Steiner, 'After the Book', in his *On Difficulty and Other Essays* (Oxford, 1980), pp. 186–203.

with stereos blasting and televisions flickering at the margins of their perception. The television screen, the picture and the caption triumph.

This thesis is exaggerated. Bookishness is not being destroyed by couch-potato culture. For some social groups, especially the urban professional middle classes, books and electronic media are not mutually substitutable; they serve quite different functions and are both valued accordingly. Others, especially the housebound, are more indifferent about both media, and yet they consider television and radio and books of roughly equal importance. Still others find that their taste for books is buoyant, if highly variable through time. A culture of reflection through bookreading is nowhere dying. In the United States, for example, the expansion of the chain bookstores, rooted in the post-war migration to the suburbs, has ensured that bestsellers that might once have sold a few hundred thousand copies now sell a million or more. The unexpected and astounding success of such books as Umberto Eco's *The Name of the Rose*, Oliver Sacks's *The Man Who Mistook His Wife for a Hat* or Paul Kennedy's *The Rise and Fall of the Great Powers*, and the even greater success of Stephen Hawking's *A Brief History of Time* (purchased by more than a million Americans), suggests a robust yearning by large numbers of readers to exercise greater control over what they read, and to confront the world through the complexity found only in books.[160]

In the same way, the recent proliferation in Europe and elsewhere of publications by and about women has helped to crystallize and to expand a feminist sensibility.

---

[160] Jason Epstein, 'The Decline and Rise of Publishing', *The New York Review of Books* (1 March 1990), pp. 8–12.

During the past two decades, for example, networks of small publishing houses run by women – the Women's Press, Virago, Pandora, Sheba, Onlywomen – have contributed greatly to the sense of non-hierarchical or horizontal difference upon which democracy thrives. These publishers have not simply helped reform the attitudes and policies of the publishing industry as a whole. Among other things, they have challenged the sexist practices of mainstream literature, promoted the work of Afro-Caribbean and Asian women and lesbian writers, led the way in revising literary history and made accessible to reading publics new bodies of difficult, 'uncommercial', radical women's literature. This important impact upon civil society of publishing 'by women, for women' is likely to survive the current financial squeeze upon independent publishers trapped in tightening markets by expanding conglomerates.

Finally, it is important to note that information storms are an inevitable feature of democratic societies. Under enduring dictatorships (Franco's Spain or Husák's Czechoslovakia are recent examples) things are quite different. Time appears to stand still. Even though individuals continue to be born, grow up, fall in love, quarrel, have children and die, everything around them becomes motionless, petrified and repetitious. Life is utterly boring. Individuals nod off into a 'permanent siesta' (Bastos). In fully democratic systems, by contrast, everything is in perpetual motion. The vigorous and the unexpected love democracy. Citizens are catapulted by their liberty into a state of permanent unease. They sense the abnormality of normality; they are capable of appreciating and tolerating a multitude of norms, of acting other than normally. The unity of purpose and compulsory sense of community of pre-democratic societies snap. There is difference, openness and constant competition among power groups to produce and to control the definition of reality. Hence, there is always an abundance of information flows. And there are public scandals, which unfold when publics learn about events which had been kept secret because, if made public in advance, they could not have been carried out.

All this is unavoidable and proper; for the chief and unsurpassed advantage of democracy is not that it guarantees peace and quiet and good decisions, but that it offers citizens the right to judge (and to reconsider their judgements about) the quality of those decisions. Democracy is rule by publics who make judgements in public. That is why the public service model defended in this essay is not a recipe for creating a heaven of communication on earth. It would in practice not put a stop to public controversies about the meaning and scope of 'liberty of the press'. Freedom of communication is not something which can be realized in a definitive or perfect sense. It is an ongoing project without an ultimate solution. It is a project which constantly generates new constellations of dilemmas and contradictions. Dworkin has pointed out, correctly, but in opposition to his own absolutist belief in 'rights', that freedom of communication is therefore jeopardized by cost-benefit analyses and the forlorn search for general and substantive rules for deciding particular disputes about the scope and meaning of 'liberty of the press'.[161] A fully democratic society guaranteed by public service media will surely suffer from ongoing

---

[161] Ronald Dworkin, 'Devaluing Liberty', *Index on Censorship*, vol. 17, no. 8 (September 1988), pp. 7–8.

'jurisdictional conflicts',[162] such as whether broadcasting should be controlled locally or defined territorially or based upon relatively homogeneous ethnic, cultural, economic or political identities. There will be ongoing debates about pornography or about the extent to which 'adult' or 'indecent' programmes should be scheduled in the late evenings, or about what constitutes seditious or libellous speech. To what extent should corporate speech and advertising-funded media be permitted? From time to time, it would severely test citizens' shared sense of the 'unreality' of reality, of the chronic instability of their societies, to the point where they may even crave for the restoration of certainty and order based on the *suppression* of certain opinions. Should computer bulletin boards be subjected to legal interference? Is a statutory right of reply of citizens against their media representatives a good thing? Should freedom of expression across nation-state frontiers be constitutionally guaranteed? Are there occasions when freedom of expression serves to reduce freedom of expression? Is the grip of television loosening? To imagine a world free of questions of this kind and unencumbered by debates over what may or may not be published, transmitted, read, seen or heard is like imagining a society without politics: all the people in it would have to be dead. In democratic societies, the scope and meaning of 'liberty of the press' and the process of representation will always be contentious, whereas a society that is drugged on either money or political authority, and which contains no controversies over

---

[162] On jurisdictional conflicts see Robert A. Dahl, *Dilemmas of Pluralist Democracy: Autonomy vs. Control* (New Haven and London, 1982), p. 85.

freedom of expression and representation, is a society that is surely dying, or dead.

The Future?

As for the future, your task is not to foresee but to enable.

Antoine de Saint-Exupéry, 1939

It may be that the United States, Britain, Germany, Italy and other countries are in the process of becoming such societies. Perhaps the market liberal chatter about choice and freedom will prove to be a stopover in the mountains on a long road which winds down into a valley of privatized serfdom. It may be that too few people will appreciate that the current reorganization of the media will do more over time to shape irreversibly the future of our societies than all the rest of 'deregulation' put together. Perhaps many opponents of market liberalism will remain half-blind. Perhaps they will fail to see that privatization of the means of communication under tighter state control is a qualitatively more serious and dangerous matter than the selling off of gas, airlines, electricity or parking meters, precisely because it is likely to penetrate the heart of everyday life – reshaping our language, our sense of time and space, our basic likes and loves. It may be that citizens will no longer invest any hopes in public life. Perhaps they will amuse themselves to death, spending their spare time 'grazing' the new abundance of pre-censored, commercialized radio, television, newspapers and magazines. Perhaps they will be persuaded to privatize themselves, to regard politics as a nuisance, to transform themselves silently and unprotestingly from citizens to mobile and private consumers. Perhaps they will forget that the media of any society are among the most important institutions – and that the courage and independence they display are always a register of the state of morale and vigour of other bodies, from schools, trade unions and churches to legislatures, governments and courts of justice. It could be that cries of 'liberty of the press' will never again be heard on the streets of London or Paris or Berlin or New York. Perhaps Tom Paine, Thomas Erskine and other old friends of freedom of communication will once again be judged guilty and forgotten – forever.

Index